T0326986

Fugitive Freedom

The publisher and the University of California Press Foundation gratefully acknowledge the generous support of the Peter Booth Wiley Endowment Fund in History.

Fugitive Freedom

THE IMPROBABLE LIVES OF TWO IMPOSTORS IN LATE COLONIAL MEXICO

William B. Taylor

UNIVERSITY OF CALIFORNIA PRESS

University of California Press
Oakland, California

© 2021 by William B. Taylor

Library of Congress Cataloging-in-Publication Data

Names: Taylor, William B., author.
Title: Fugitive freedom : the improbable lives of two impostors in late
   colonial Mexico / William B. Taylor.
Description: Oakland, California : University of California Press, [2021] |
   Includes bibliographical references and index.
Identifiers: LCCN 2020025987 (print) | LCCN 2020025988 (ebook) |
   ISBN 9780520368569 (cloth) | ISBN 9780520976146 (ebook)
Subjects: LCSH: Aguayo y Herrera, Joseph Lucas, 1747- | Atondo, Juan,
   1783?- | Catholic Church—Mexico—History—18th century. | Impostors
   and imposture—Mexico—18th century. | Church and state—Mexico—
   History—18th century. | Mexico—Church history—18th century.
Classification: LCC HV6761.M62 A487 2021 (print) | LCC HV6761.M62
   (ebook) | DDC 364.16/33092272—dc23
LC record available at https://lccn.loc.gov/2020025987
LC ebook record available at https://lccn.loc.gov/2020025988

Manufactured in the United States of America

30 29 28 27 26 25 24 23 22 21
10 9 8 7 6 5 4 3 2 1

Contents

List of Maps

Preface

One of the first books I read about Mexican history was Norman Martin's *Los vagabundos en la Nueva España: Siglo XVI* (1957). To this novice historian of Latin America, it was a tantalizing point of entry into law and disorder. According to the decrees and commentary by Spanish viceroys and judges Martin cited, wandering strangers, paupers, impostors, and other cheaters speckled the countryside and loitered in cities throughout the sixteenth century, stirring up trouble. But his sources were silent on who the wanderers were, how they came to live as they did, what they cared about, and what their intentions were. Were they just an annoyance, or did they pose a serious threat to colonial society and public morals? Were there broad social changes stirring beneath the steady stream of decrees and administrative campaigns against them? Could their stories reveal something I was missing about the course of early Latin American history? The closest I could come in my reading to a life like these was Periquillo Sarniento, Mexico's famous fictional *pícaro*, conjured by José Joaquín Fernández de Lizardi in 1816.

Finding that Martin's colonial *vagabundos* were as elusive in the written record as they were on the ground, I moved on to better-documented subjects that promised to answer some of my questions about colonization and Latin America in formation: land systems, social and political life of colonial Indian villages, priests in their parishes, shrines, the material culture of devotion. Yet *vagabundos* and other people out of place kept me wondering what I was missing about the temper of the times and the social order.

This book introduces two colonial *vagabundos*, Joseph Aguayo and Juan Atondo, both of them small-time troublemakers and priest impersonators in central Mexico during the last decades of Spanish rule. Impersonating a priest was a serious crime against the state religion and its institutions that was sure to attract the Inquisition's attention, especially if the impersonator had jeopardized penitents' prospects for salvation by pretending to confess and absolve them of their sins. The written record for Aguayo and Atondo is unusually rich, offering an opportunity to approach the personal histories and inner lives of two people at the margins of polite society. Doing so, and also examining others' relationships to them, enlarges an understanding of colonial—and, indeed, transoceanic—history by, first, recognizing that "the Spanish colonial order" was unfinished from the start, always coming apart as well as coming together, and, second, complicating prevailing social and spiritual ideals with the plebeian underworlds that haunted the imaginations of state builders throughout the colonial period. The lives and appetites of these two characters reminded me, and perhaps themselves, of Hispanic literary *pícaros* like Periquillo and the seminal Guzmán de Alfarache, but they were different, too, in some ways that still reflected a long-prevailing mood in Spanish and colonial Spanish American society of *engaño* and a wary suspicion that most people, especially in this New World, were not who they appeared to be.

There have always been cheaters, liars, charlatans, and impostors, and I suppose many of us have been tempted to pull a fast one for personal advantage, but there are times when the big lies, misrepresentations, and impersonations are more pervasive, or at least more notorious. Europe and its dominions during the sixteenth, seventeenth, and eighteenth centuries—the Early Modern Period—was one of those times. (For example, in her 2012 book *Renaissance Impostors and Proofs of Identity*, Miriam Eliav-Feldon finds Europe then teeming with impostors.) While my purpose is not to explain this widespread opening for impostors in the Early Modern Period or how great disruptions and political and social changes then laid the foundation for even more frequent and outrageous impostures since the eighteenth century, the subject prompts hard questions that need to be kept in mind. Did the sweeping dislocations in the sixteenth century drive people who might otherwise have led commonplace lives to risk making their way by deception and betrayal? Or is it more that state builders and the public were especially alert to imposture then, and intent on enforcing order, uncertain about whether self-serving opportunists on the fringes of society were merely scoundrels or truly wicked and dangerous? Was the late eighteenth century, when Aguayo and Atondo lived, a time of more impostors and swindlers in Mexico? Perhaps not, and there are reasons to think that authorities then were more on the lookout for them and other lawbreakers.

There are no simple answers to these historical questions, or indeed to the psychosocial question of why impostors succeed, at least for a time. But they are compelling questions to me because we also live in unsettled times, erupting with fear of strangers in our lives who harbor schemes for private gain, attention, and political advantage, and with talk-show hosts cautioning their listeners that "everything you're seeing is deception" (present company excepted). There are internet bots let loose to spread lies and fear, replete with images Photoshopped to mislead; fraudulent attempts to obtain sensitive information from people who merely answer the phone or check their email; and swindlers on a grand personal scale. Included in that last group are Ponzi schemer Bernard Madoff; Elizabeth Holmes and her bogus blood-testing device; Dr. Paolo Macchiarini with his deadly synthetic trachea implants and fantastic lies to his wife and lovers; would-be socialite Anna (Sorokin) Delvey, who lived the high life in New York by deceiving wealthy acquaintances and employees of luxury hotels; and Enric Marco, who for decades basked in the reputation of a Holocaust survivor and Spanish Civil War hero.

Times of turbulent, systemic change bring opportunity as well as loss to the desperate and daring, giving rise to an abundance of shady opportunists who prey on the credulous with something to lose. Prevailing outlooks in such times are diffuse and hard to pin down, but they bend the local history of every impostor and his or her audience in ways that can sometimes raise an ordinary fraudster to wider notoriety. An outlook of the time and place that brought Aguayo and Atondo to light and both enabled and limited their success is an elusive subtext of this book.

Fugitive Freedom is meant to stand on its own as a scholarly work, but it was written with history readers more broadly in mind, including students in college courses about early Latin America. The priceless friendship of fellow teachers, scholars, and curators who nourished the project belies the worlds of deceit and despair from which it springs. This time, a long conversation with Kenneth Mills early in the research, his many helpful observations, and a wonderfully detailed evaluation of the manuscript kept me on course. Sylvia Sellers-García, Brianna Leavitt-Alcántara, Katrina Olds, and Allen Wells also read a draft and kindly shared ideas and key questions that gave me pause and pointed toward answers. David Carrasco, Margaret Chowning, Brian Connaughton, Ilona Katzew, Sarah López, Alicia Mayer González, Sean McEnroe, Karen Melvin, Mieko Nishida, Paul Ramírez, Gretchen Starr-LeBeau, Jorge Traslosheros, and Nicole Von Germeten also took an interest in the project and offered encouragement. Once again, Nancy D. Mann brought her critical skills, curiosity, and wide learning to bear on my writing.

Walter Brem reminded me of Juan Atondo's trial record in the Bancroft Library, and José Adrián Barragán Álvarez made a digital copy available. Brian Connaughton and his research assistant, Angélica Hoyos García, helped track down the scattered parts of trial records for Joseph Aguayo in the Archivo General de la Nación in Mexico City. The libraries of Bowdoin, Bates, and Colby Colleges provided many of the secondary sources I needed to begin to see the subject in context.

Kate Marshall went beyond her duties as an acquisitions editor at the University of California Press to imagine the book and help make it better, Enrique Ochoa-Kaup and Francisco Reinking helped see it through to completion, and Lindsey Westbrook was my excellent copy editor. Bill Nelson Cartographic Services prepared the maps. Epigraphs quoting James Tate and Inga Clendinnen are used with the permission of Wesleyan University Press and Giramondo Publishing Co., respectively.

Special thanks to Dylan Joy, archivist in the Benson Latin American Collection at the University of Texas at Austin and to Tom Lisanti and Andrea Felder in Permissions and Reproduction Services of the New York Public Library for their help on short notice with reproductions of the cover image.

Translations from Spanish to English are mine unless a published translation is noted, which is usually the case for *La vida de*

Lazarillo de Tormes, Francisco de Quevedo's *La vida del buscón,* and Fernández de Lizardi's *El Periquillo Sarniento.* I rely especially on David Frye's fine, often pungent translations of these three novels, after comparing his passages against the original Spanish. Michael Alpert's lively translation of Quevedo's novel was irresistible in one instance.

Dedicated to my former student colleagues in Denver, Boulder, Guadalajara, Charlottesville, Dallas, and Berkeley

Introduction

"The sixteenth century lives in terror of the tramp."

—R. H. TAWNEY[1]

Taking the measure of Latin American history from Christopher Columbus's voyages to the movements for national independence in the early nineteenth century has mainly meant attending to Europe's conquests and what took shape thereafter. To Hugh Thomas, in four thick volumes, it meant Spain's rise to greatness as a world power in the sixteenth century—relentless exploration, conquest, and mastery of territory and peoples.[2] This is history with direction, guided by outsize history makers riding a cresting wave of riches in American gold and silver—not just *conquistadores*, but also sixteenth-century monarchs Charles V and Philip II and their agents, who went about building the first global empire "by the sword and the compass, more and more and more and more," as a Spanish chronicler put it in 1599.[3] Late in his long reign, Philip II was tasked with beating back freebooters and rival European states from Spain's colonial shores as expansion gave way to consolidation and defense in what Thomas called "the age of administration," a subject he left to others.

But as Sean McEnroe writes, "Despite the arrogance of colonial maps and flags, it is far from easy to describe how empires were built, controlled, and bounded."[4] In a less triumphal spirit than Thomas, other historians surveying the first centuries of Latin America have looked more closely at what was being built and lost, and found more protagonists, victims, rebels, resilience, structures, and ambiguous processes. Institutions and systems of empire were taking shape, with an outpouring of new law and an elaborate bureaucracy of governors, councils, judges, tax collectors, constables, and clergymen. Merchant capital on a global scale was beginning to shape the colonial economy, and great wealth was being extracted and spent by the state and classes of privileged colonists, while millions of indigenous subjects died of epidemic diseases and abuse. African slaves and new forms of coerced labor were substituted where they were needed to keep production of lucrative exports flowing. Slaves, peasants, and debt laborers suffered horribly, yet sometimes succeeded in subverting their masters' plans for them. Cities developed (often beginning as administrative centers), as did mining operations and landed estates. Colonial society became a labyrinth of ethnicities, family trees, wealth, royal favor, talent, and convenience: Old Christian Spaniards (Iberians whose ancestors had been Christians since "beyond living memory") and those who claimed Spanish ancestry, nobles, merchants, landlords, priests, governors, bureaucrats, landed *pueblos de indios*, mestizos, *mulatos*, and others who did not fit comfortably into the recognized racial groupings of Spaniards, Indians, and Blacks. Men and women of all social backgrounds who were not so obviously looped into positions of power and public life made history, too, however inconspicuously. Historians have arranged the development of all these groups and structures together along lines of demographic change, race, class, inequality, gender, violence, struggle, alliance, accommodation, acquiescence, and survival that describe what Latin America was becoming and why the Spanish and Portuguese empires lasted as long as they did. They turn out to be less closed regimes of a ruling elite than was once supposed—less ruled by force, less smooth running, and often more pragmatic.[5]

Whether the teller orders this story as a pageant of conquest and global empire or a mosaic of contingent power and scattered agency, surveys of the three centuries of colonial history tend to emphasize the sixteenth century as the formative period, when Hapsburg political power over the Iberian kingdoms was consolidated and the institutions and cultural habits of early Latin America seemed to stabilize, even crystallize.[6] Muffled by these great themes are the widespread, long-term disruptions, displacements, and impoverishment in the midst of plenty that contemporary commentators recognized as threats to public order and to Spain's predominance in Europe and overseas.

It is easy to forget that a sense of things coming apart was rooted in this history from the beginning, and that colonization of even the wealthiest New World territories was unfinished, limited by resources and means of communication, at risk from within as much as from foreign threats.[7] How would the many kinds of people physically displaced or unfamiliar and under suspicion—now strangers in their land—be managed and absorbed into Iberian colonial societies? And how could those societies meet the perpetual clamor of descendants of the *conquistadores* and other impatient Spaniards in the Americas who expected to live off government appointments, sinecures, and the labor and resources of native retainers and debtors? There were new policies and efforts at enforcement, but colonial rule remained a work in progress right to the end. *Fugitive Freedom* tells of two restless, self-centered young men from the ragged edges of polite society shortly before Mexican independence who, in making their way, disturbed everyday life around them and alarmed colonial officials with their deceptions and lies.

Strangers in the Land: Prosperity, Poverty, Expansion, and Displacement in Spain and New Spain

Spain and the rest of Christian Europe in the sixteenth century were engulfed by the rupture of a single Christian church of the West centered in Rome, as the rise of Protestant denominations attached to rival states and regions splintered communities, states, and the Holy Roman Empire. The Roman Catholic Church looked especially to Spain for financial and political support as it reformed and eventually went on the offensive in the seventeenth century, often with members of the Jesuit order in the lead. The merging of smaller states into incipient nations and the flow of edicts, broadsides, forms, pamphlets, religious texts, and books of all sorts printed from movable type made for an administrative revolution, with new institutions and an elaborate bureaucracy to oversee far-flung territories and many subjects. Rome increasingly found itself attempting to orchestrate a collection of provincial and proto-national churches, themselves undergoing their own substantial institutional and liturgical reforms, guided by the decrees of the Council of Trent. As in the state reforms, the accent was on order, hierarchy, competence, and direction from above—seminaries and missals for the priesthood, catechism and confession for the laity. American wealth and millions of unconverted or new Christian subjects added to the challenges and opportunities for Spain as an imperial power and standard-bearer of the Catholic Church in this time of division, reconstruction, and expansion.

For many Spaniards, there was a steep social cost in the dramatic developments of the sixteenth century: state building and union of kingdoms, strengthening of ties to the Holy Roman Empire and the Catholic Church, incessant warfare, the halting rise of merchant capitalism and the fortunes made by privileged families, headlong expansion in and beyond Europe, and inflowing wealth of precious metals and high-value spices, dyestuffs, silk, sugar, chocolate, and tobacco from new overseas possessions. One measure of the cost was widespread displacement of people, social orphanhood, and often impoverishment and early death. Despite the population growth of the early sixteenth century, Spain began to experience labor shortages and turned increasingly to penal servitude at home and slavery and labor drafts in the colonies. Several hundred thousand Castilian and Aragonese men out of a population of about eight million volunteered or were pressed into service in Spain's foreign wars during the sixteenth and early seventeenth centuries, not to mention the expulsion of tens of thousands of Jews in the 1490s and the departure after 1609 of Spain's remaining Muslims. Many Spanish citizen soldiers who survived the battles in Italy, central Europe, the Low Countries, and the Indies returned to join the floating population of destitute country folk moving to cities that were ill prepared to accommodate them all.[8] And many wanderers, without gainful employment or the support of nearby relatives, found lives on the road as peddlers, prostitutes, beggars, itinerant laborers, thieves, or worse. Several hundred thousand more left for Spanish colonies in the Americas and Asia. Droughts and an epidemic in the 1590s that swept away close to half a million Castilians drove others off the land, as did the Mesta, the powerful organization of sheepmen running their herds through village farmlands and orchards, and retarding the textile industry in the cities of Spain's tableland by exporting their wool.[9] How to hold together and manage this churning, emergent Spanish nation-state and vast empire of strangers in an age of sail, draft animals, quill pens, and scarce, costly paper? How to establish order in places swelling with people speaking different languages and practicing different religions? How to deal with all the vagabonds and other people adrift without a home or a certain identity? In political and social terms, unification meant putting people in their place, within a Catholic state and social categories, and enforcing royal decrees through constabularies and courts. Jews and Muslims had to convert or leave Spain. Likewise in the empire, to qualify as the king's subjects rather than enemies, "pagans" had to become at least nominal Christians. Segregation laws followed, meant to restrict most marriages to couples of the same ethnic designation—*español*, Indian, or Black—and to keep non-Indians out of colonial *pueblos de indios*. Religion was a fundamental instrument of unification, but the lingering suspicion that converts were weak and tepid Christians who would revert to old ways and undermine the True Faith led directly to new distinctions and barriers. Old Christians were favored for royal preferments and access to professional careers. Since the dubious new Christians were descendants of Jews, North African Muslims, indigenous peoples of the colonies, and sub-Saharan African slaves—people of "impure blood"—their progeny were tainted by their new Christian ancestry as well as by the suspicion that they, or their near ancestors, were born out of wedlock.

Judging by the number of royal and municipal edicts, theological treatises, and other political and religious commentaries in

Spain and Spanish America about people out of place, vagabonds and paupers from elsewhere emerged as a social type and were seen as an especially serious challenge to social and moral order, alongside witches, gypsies, and madmen.[10] One commentator at the turn of the seventeenth century estimated one hundred and fifty thousand *vagabundos* in Spain; another in the 1690s guessed that twenty thousand more turned up every year, many of them from foreign countries.[11] These numbers are crude estimates, but a chorus of political commentators across three centuries sounded the alarm that vagabonds were a serious threat. The distinguished mid-seventeenth-century jurist Juan de Solórzano y Pereira, who had a foot in America as well as one in Spain, claimed that "swarms of beggars are to be found everywhere in this Kingdom. In no other part of the world will one find so many legions of beggars as in Spain," a sentiment echoed in the late eighteenth century by Bernardo Ward.[12]

That there were large and growing numbers of displaced people is clear, but can we take at face value contemporary officials' claim that there was a plague of undeserving poor and demented on the loose in the cities and on the roads, undermining peace and good order? Poverty was not new, and in the past it had seemed intractable, inevitable. It was more visible and disruptive now partly because there were more outcasts, but also because they clustered in the larger cities and along commercial routes. The new attention to poverty and vagrancy also reflected the interests and aspirations of ambitious state builders in Spain determined to impose order on a larger scale. Policy makers at court and in the provinces, in their optimism and newfound power, thought that the solution to both the old and the (apparently) new problem lay in administrative action—new laws and enforcement.[13]

The Spanish kingdoms in Iberia and beyond were not the only places where vagabonds and beggars attracted official attention, charitable and otherwise. Every European state and affiliated church moved to provide for the deserving poor and contain and punish those who were seen as outside idlers and paupers, presumed to be troublemakers. The measures taken by authorities at the municipal level and above were as much or more about control and alarm as they were about charity. England is especially well known for its Poor Laws and Vagabond Acts from 1497 through the eighteenth century. As Henry VIII saw it, idleness was the mother and root of all vices. At first, English vagabonds and idlers were required to spend three nights in the stocks for a first offense and then sent back to their former homes. By the 1530s and 1540s, the truly needy and helpless had to be licensed in order to beg, and could do so only in a designated part of town. Vagabonds could be whipped, given two years of penal servitude, and branded with a V for a first offense, and executed if arrested a second time. By the 1570s, these penalties for "sturdy beggars" were accompanied by royal laws to reduce begging and provide relief for the deserving local poor by imposing a new tax on parish residents and proposing to establish houses of correction and workhouses to put the poor to work, especially in spinning and weaving.[14]

Early Spanish Poor Laws in 1540 and 1565 may have been less severe in their prescribed punishments—calling for exile and occasionally short periods of forced labor and floggings for repeat offenders—but they were similar in intent and spirit to the English laws in seeking to identify the truly needy local paupers and clamp down on all others—aiming to remove poor and idle strangers, especially from cities, by registering the deserving poor and licensing them to beg only in their hometowns. The laws placed beggars and vagabonds in the same class as mortal sinners—gamblers, prostitutes, and others requiring firm correction and improvement. Ascribed ravenous appetites for rich food and drink, and boundless greed for money, they lived "like barbarians" and did not attend Mass, confess, or take communion.[15] Accordingly, from 1565 into the eighteenth century, Spanish reforms and regulations centered on hospitals, sanctuaries, hospital orders such as the Order of San Juan de Dios, charitable confraternities, alms, and other private contributions, as well as on more punishment and organized policing with new *alguaciles de vagabundos* (constables in charge of vagabonds) to enforce the exile and penal laws.[16]

This attention to jobless vagabonds on the roads and moving to cities and towns was echoed in correspondence and edicts of viceregal officials in Mexico throughout the colonial period. As early as 1565 a judge on the high court in Mexico City advised Philip II that vagabonds "are as many as the weeds and grow in number every day." Fifteen years later, Viceroy Martín Enríquez lamented the many "vagabonds without occupation, who serve no one" and needed to be kept out of Indian villages.[17] Initially, it was wandering Spanish immigrants without government preferments who were regarded as the dangerous thieves, highway robbers, exploiters of Indian villagers in remote places, and generally lowlife (*mala vida*) characters. As time passed, the main concern became other kinds of rootless strangers: vagrants, peddlers, and impostors whom officials often took to be *mestizos* and *mulatos*, people who doubly did not belong since they were neither Spaniards, nor Indians, nor Blacks.[18] Perhaps to an even greater degree than in Spain, colonial governors and judges emphasized punishment of vagrants more than an organized program of removal and charity, which was left largely to the Church and lay brotherhoods.

With the growth of regional cities, *hospicios de pobres* (asylums for the needy and helpless), hospitals, and other charitable institutions, colonial authorities writing about the idle poor sounded more like their peninsular counterparts, attending to urban beggars as well as *vagabundos*. In the eighteenth century, rural policing became a priority and again *vagabundos* were singled out for attention. In the words of the royal instruction to the viceroy of New Spain in 1739, it was time to "cleanse the republic of vagabonds and lowlife people . . . since such people only serve to corrupt good customs, introduce wicked ways, and commit crimes."[19] Corporal punishment and forced labor were the accepted remedies. Most late-colonial convicted *vagabundos* were sentenced to textile sweatshops, coastal fortifications, and public works, while service on sugar plantations or in bakeries or tanneries was sometimes ordered for *negros* and *mulatos*. Especially harsh sentences were meted out to armed *vagabundos*, and highway robbers convicted of murder could expect a death sentence.[20]

But even with all the official attention to *vagabundos* and paupers, it is hard to say who they were, beyond where they were found and what they were accused of. Contemporary commentators in Spain tended to focus on seven types of disreputable idlers and vagrants from away: *vagamundos*, those who "wandered the world," masterless and not known locally; medical quacks, who also sometimes posed as priests and told tall tales about having escaped captivity by some miraculous means; wandering priests, whether ordained or impostors; gypsies; deserters from the military; those who faked illness; and men who impersonated fathers and exploited their "children" for personal gain. But these are types, not particular cases. It is mainly in the literary figure of the insouciant *pícaro* that shifty vagrants and hustlers emerge from the shadows as individuals more than stock characters, with histories and personalities.

Identifying factors that made for many displaced people and wanderers in Early Modern Spain and the Americas is not difficult, but establishing their relative importance in place and time, and going beyond broad generalizations, is a greater, unfinished challenge. And the evidence—mainly directives by officials, theological debates, laws, legal commentaries, and records of charitable institutions—would seem to say more about the perceptions and intentions of elites than about the beggars and vagabonds. Those historians who see the wanderers as forlorn economic migrants have considered poverty the important factor, even when Spain was riding high in the sixteenth century. For them, misery—from natural disaster or budding commercial capitalism, the Mesta, and war—drove the wretched toward Toledo, Madrid, Zaragoza, Barcelona, Córdoba, Granada, and Sevilla, cities that seemed to promise new opportunities even if they were administrative centers more than engines of production and exchange. But by the late sixteenth century, when the crown was defaulting on foreign loans and facing huge expenses for defense of the empire, most cities had less to offer new arrivals, as prices rose and the royal treasury extracted loans, taxed cities to the hilt, and tripled the *alcabala* sales tax. Many urban migrants who remained found themselves without gainful employment. Others took to the road.[21]

Some writers of the time suggested that most of the wandering migrants were foreigners, including Moorish and Turkish spies who had crossed into Spain to prey on the bighearted charity of Spanish Catholics.[22] As Gabriel Pérez del Barrio put it in 1697, foreigners "enter in a naked state and before a year is out they leave covered in enough gold and silver to last them two years," and their presence threatened to corrupt Catholics with their heresies and superstitions.[23] Christian tradition and the Catholic doctrine of works no doubt encouraged alms giving, which redeemed the donor through the pauper,[24] but the idea of an invasion of foreign loafers, schemers, and spies probably was rooted in a mounting suspicion of unassimilated gypsies and *moriscos* (descendants of Iberian and North African Muslims who converted to Christianity), and Spain's military setbacks and declining hegemony in Europe beyond the Mediterranean.

More likely than an invasion of foreign migrants, it was rising expectations, combined with natural disasters, hunger, and want, that moved many thousands of sixteenth-century Spaniards into cities where new wealth and amenities were on display, or to distant colonial shores that supplied much of the fabled riches. As a fictional immigrant in Peru put it in the early seventeenth century, he went there seeking "respectability and renown, and all that the Indies promise."[25] More of the Spaniards who left home for the Americas would have been economic refugees in the seventeenth century, when prolonged economic decline gripped Spain and much of Europe, but even then the exodus was also fed by hopes of making or taking a share of America's wealth and living an *hidalgo's* pretensions to nobility and a privileged life of ease and authority.[26]

A World of Appearances and Suspicion

The great changes of the time were cultural as well as political, economic, and social, and the impulse to incorporate and impose order where order was in doubt was shaped in good part by Spain's expansion overseas and the prominent place of reformed Catholicism in all aspects of peninsular and colonial life, both as a state religion and as a popular and personal faith. The ways imagined by Spain's leaders to make one people and one faith in these chaotic times split into binary choices. Philip II was clear that he would rather not rule at all than rule over infidels.[27] Memory of a tradition of coexistence and tolerance among peoples was not erased, but it was overshadowed in civic and religious life by stark choices between conversion and exile.[28]

Such polar oppositions were framed in a hardening Counter-Reformation vocabulary: impurity and purity; the corrupt body and the immortal soul; evil and goodness; Satan and Christ, both of them powerfully present in the world; darkness and light; moon and sun; convert and Old Christian; and, in cynicism and satire, *engaño* (deception) and *desengaño* (disabuse and disillusionment). The religious outlook of the time also tapped into an ecstatic vein of Christianity that, by means of direct union with God, promised another way to transcend the temptations and corruptions of the here and now. At the same time, there were gnawing doubts about the outcome of these struggles between opposing forces: that Satan might be winning the contest for souls, that many people were not who they seemed to be, that the *conversos, moriscos,* and new Christians overseas were counterfeit Christians. Impostors seemed to be everywhere, posing as priests, pious hermits, mystics, beggars, royal officials, and physicians. Others lived out sinful, secret lives as bigamists, sexual deviants, and priests soliciting women in the confessional. Strangers to the law and the community—vagabonds, people of mixed race, and other newcomers of all kinds—harbored sinister intentions. The doctrine of original sin, belief in the devil as a palpable presence rather than a frothy metaphor, and a climate of secrecy represented by the confessional fostered distrust of people who violated norms or did not fit comfortably into established social categories.[29] In this shifting world of appearances, in which sin, deception, and betrayal seemed at hand, the literary *pícaro* came to stand for the undeserving, but possibly redeemable poor—wayward, idle, cheeky, an amoral liar poised to trick, steal, and disturb.

Gliding past the common conviction that everyone was inclined toward the picaresque by way of original sin, and that evasion, however polite, was dishonest and hypocritical, some Spanish reformers of the time dichotomized another salient distinction: simulation (imposture) and dissimulation (prudent concealment). These writers treated simulation and dissimulation as different kinds of deception, with simulation as the evil twin.[30] Simulation—to feign something that does not exist—was a form of deceit that Spanish commentators attributed especially to the lower reaches of society, including *pícaros* and the sturdy beggars and strangers that early Poor Laws singled out for discipline. To dissimulate, on the other hand, was not really to lie. It could be a morally grounded, positive kind of pretense in which actors protected their own well-being and the well-being of others, allowing different beliefs and attitudes to coexist unacknowledged for their mutual benefit. Faced with shifting loyalties and base motives, it was often necessary.[31]

Jesuit Baltasar Gracián's mid-seventeenth-century collection of maxims for "the art of living," *Oráculo manual y arte de prudencia*, exemplifies this endorsement of dissimulation—framed, to avoid censure by the Inquisition, as oblique advice that the reader must interpret.[32] Discretion, self-control, guarded circumspection, and humility are the keys to Gracián's guide to happiness and success in a world of appearances and perilous uncertainties. Control your emotions, and be agreeable, wary, flexible, and circumspect, he advised. Deflect flattery, be careful what you disclose, recognize when you need to conceal your true feelings, and seek balance, moderation, and accommodation. Above all, expect to constantly readjust your position as circumstances change, and avoid excesses of all kinds.[33] Here are five of his maxims for the aspiring dissimulator: (1) Don't say too much; don't speak in superlatives. (2) Don't claim everything or refuse everything. . . . Those who want everything for themselves do not know how to give ground even in the smallest matter, nor to share any comfort or convenience. Others give up everything. There is always stupidity in excesses, and here it has an unhappy result. These people do not have even an hour to themselves. . . . No one seeks them out except when they want something from them. (3) All victories breed hate, and a victory over your superior is foolish or fatal. (4) Don't humiliate others. "Who gives much does not give, but sells." Don't drain gratitude to the dregs, for when recipients see that all return is impossible, they break off the relationship. (5) Always act as if you are being observed.

Maxims like these were not new, but they were being articulated in Spain more clearly and more often, from more quarters, than before and they were as common in the eighteenth century as earlier. One example of this deep and widespread mistrust of appearances and expectation of deception comes from the *Historia del Huérfano* (History of the Orphan), a novel of restless travels, religious calling, and a lonely quest for deserved recognition by its righteous protagonist. Apparently completed in 1621, it was written by a Spanish Augustinian friar who spent most of his life in Peru. The novel's hero extols true, steadfast friendship, quoting Erasmus: "A friend is more essential than fire and water, but for few does it come their way."[34] What he finds, however, is a world of false friends.

Two Impostors

I cannot answer many of the basic historical questions about these troublesome *vagabundos* and impostors—how many drifters and swindlers there were in Spain and New Spain at various points in time, where they were found, what led them to keep on as they did. My more accessible goal is to draw closer to two Mexican men who lived the inequalities, risks, and opportunities of New Spain in this way: who they were, what they did over a number of years, what they valued, how they presented themselves to authorities and the public, and how they were regarded. Joseph Aguayo and Juan Atondo were outcasts, on the move and on the make near the end of Spanish rule in mainland America. Neither one was famous in his time. As far as I know, this is their first appearance in the written history of Latin America.

Aguayo and Atondo are especially tempting subjects because of the written record by and about them. It offers an opportunity to learn in some detail about their lives of duplicity, misadventure, and atonement in central Mexico and beyond. They appear over time in these records, rather than in one tantalizing incident or utterance, with glimpses of them as boys and then again as young men and older adults, still recognizably themselves, as they appeared before the Inquisition and were called to describe and account for what they had done. Personal qualities show through— evasiveness and cunning in Aguayo's case, and awkwardness and ingenuousness in Atondo's. Some details of their transient lives also come out: where they went and how they lived, particular lies and deceits, and how they wished to appear in public. There is also something of their inner lives—stated and implicit motives, longings, appetites, fears, misgivings, and grudges.[35]

At a glance, Aguayo and Atondo were similar in how they made their way in the world. Both were literate and posed as priests for a time. They were self-absorbed, expedient liars, taking flight when they were about to be found out. They were arrested more than once, and were released or escaped. Both were performers, although Aguayo was more in control of the performance, mastering the deportment, speech, gesture, and posture of the character he pretended to be. They also presented themselves to the Inquisitors in more than one way, especially Aguayo. They were unfailingly respectful, but remorseful and apologetic in one appearance, in denial or deflecting responsibility with a hint of indignation in another, and, with Aguayo, in his first trial, presenting himself as too young to be fully responsible for his actions. But in the end, as I hope to show, the differences between them are more striking and revealing than the similarities.

Not all impostors attracted the attention of colonial courts, or suffered the same consequences as Aguayo and Atondo. Some who led what appear to have been more provocative and lawless lives even achieved a measure of acceptance and fame in their time. Consider Catalina de Erauso, the notorious Basque cross-dressing "lieutenant nun." Around 1600, at age fifteen, she fled her sheltered life as a novice in a Dominican convent and entered a life of restless adventure, violence, and romance as a fugitive posing as a man, first in Spain, then becoming a soldier in the king's service in Chile and Argentina and a mule driver in Mexico, where she died in 1650. According to what seems to be her autobiography, she was no stranger to gambling, hard drinking, and violence, and was a party to fighting that ended in the deaths of seven men.[36] Arrested for murder in Huamanga, Peru, she confessed her mortal sins to the bishop and informed him that she was really a woman who had taken first vows in a convent in Spain. Once it was determined that she was a virgin, Erauso was allowed to join a conventual community in Lima. Two years later she returned to Spain, where she petitioned the king for a soldier's pension for battlefield services, and later traveled to Rome, where she received permission from the pope to continue dressing as a man.

How did Erauso get away with murder while Aguayo and Atondo found little sympathy for their nonviolent crimes? Why were her mannishness and daring pardoned and even rewarded rather than treated as a threat to public order?[37] She seems to have been regarded at the time as a singular curiosity, perhaps because she displayed manly virtues at a time when Spanish military might was on the wane and doubts about Spanish manhood on the battlefield were creeping in. Erauso's audacious public campaign for recognition by the highest authorities paid off. She apparently dictated her life story three different times and commissioned portraits of herself twice in her successful petitions at Madrid and Rome. Had dozens of flamboyant Catalinas presented themselves, the state and Church probably would not have been so forgiving, but a fascination with the exceptional manly woman can be found in local folklore elsewhere in Spain and the Americas, too.[38]

Aside from her skill at self-promotion, manly prowess, service to the king, and deference to the pope, what most sets Catalina de Erauso and her destiny apart from Atondo and Aguayo is that the latter impersonated priests, which landed them in the lap of the Inquisition. This crime of posing as a priest or even as an officer of the Inquisition was not new—there had been a steady trickle of such cases since the mid-sixteenth century—but Aguayo and Atondo happened along when Inquisitors were especially touchy about threats to their authority as their power was waning, and slights to the good name of the clergy.[39] Even so, Aguayo preferred the Inquisition to the crown courts since the Bourbon monarchy's emphasis on fixed rules and law enforcement had led to new policing forces with a reputation for cruelty, squalid conditions in overcrowded and more secure royal jails, rigid application of criminal laws, and harsher sentences.[40] There was little room in these criminal courts for the extenuating circumstances and appeals for mercy and forgiveness that Aguayo hoped to employ before the Inquisition.

Thanks to the network of agents of the Holy Office and the probings of prosecuting Inquisitors in Mexico City, we have written records for Aguayo and Atondo. As rich as the records are, and from the same court, they differ in ways that reveal more about Atondo's inner life and less about his public presentation of self, his devious ways in the world, or how he may have changed in the passage from youth to adulthood. For Aguayo, there are three Inquisition trials and a bulging dossier that spans more than twenty years as he kept returning to the Inquisition's attention. For Atondo, there is a more compact set of records during the three years or so he was in the Inquisition's custody, from late 1815 to 1818. He was allowed to tell his meandering story several times at unusual length. The Inquisition's independent investigation concentrated on the months he posed as an ordained priest. Oddly, given all the personal revelations, there is little about how he expressed himself through body language, a kind of information that emerges occasionally in the record for Aguayo, who was more careful with words in his contacts with authorities and the people he deceived.

The Mexican Inquisition after 1750

The Mexican Inquisition that Aguayo and Atondo encountered in the years shortly before it was abolished for good in 1820 has yet to be studied closely, but the consensus among scholars who have touched on the subject is that this tribunal was a shadow of its former self. They emphasize that the Inquisition faced declining revenues, was drawn into trivial matters such as disputes among staff members in the Mexico City offices, and increasingly was occupied with discipline of the clergy, as is suggested by the many trials for solicitation in the confessional.[41] Otherwise, the court is thought to have centered its attention on protecting the crown's political interests, censuring subversive political literature, and gathering information on possible enemies of the state.[42]

One sign of politicization is in the records of the Mexican Inquisition's Index of forbidden books. Monelisa Pérez Marchand found that until about 1750 the Index's list looked much as it had for two centuries, consisting of works considered heretical or deviating from religious orthodoxy in some other way. After midcentury, the Index included many more works espousing revolutionary political ideas, especially the writings of French *philosophes*.[43] The court's renewed interest in converting foreign Protestants who came the Inquisition's way no doubt served the crown's interests, too. The files of investigations in the Inquisition archive in Mexico City also show that agents of the court monitored French residents in New Spain—merchants, watchmakers, pastry chefs, sailors, hairdressers, and a few clergymen and district governors—who were suspected of holding liberal political and religious ideas that challenged the monarchy or Christian doctrine and practice. In Louisiana as well, after the beginning of Spanish rule in 1763,

Inquisition agents were busy uncovering devotees of French Enlightenment thought and tracking down Masons and other freethinkers.[44]

Some of the most explosive issues taken up by the Mexican Inquisition in the sixteenth and seventeenth centuries—demonic possession, witchcraft, crypto-Judaism, and iconoclasm—received less attention in the eighteenth century and were more likely to be regarded as superstitions than intentional, malevolent, mortal sins. Other changes in the Inquisition's agenda that were meant to protect the colonial regime and contain disruptive conduct and sacrilegious skepticism included more attention to policing rowdy, irreverent behavior and sale of food and beverages at the solemn processions on High Holy Days, and confiscating profane objects like buttons and knives decorated with religious images.

The Mexican Inquisition's solemn *autos de fe* in the late eighteenth century were less fraught spectacles than their more elaborately staged seventeenth-century predecessors, which sometimes culminated in executions of condemned heretics, including those who repented their heresies at the last minute.[45] The *autos de fe* in Mexico City in 1649 and 1659 had begun with a procession of the condemned and hundreds of dignitaries on horseback, including the viceroy, and had been attended by tens of thousands of somber spectators, some up in nearby trees for a better view, many seated in bleachers built for the occasion near the elevated stage where the condemned were displayed and their crimes read out. The humiliation of the condemned continued the next day as they were paraded through the city streets on donkeys, whipped and wearing a placard that identified their offenses, which were proclaimed aloud by the town crier. The reconciliations followed, and if there was an execution, it was accompanied by musket blasts and pealing of the cathedral bells. The late eighteenth-century *autos de fe* may have been less elaborate and lacked a *quemadero* (the place of execution) as a focal point, but they were still riveting public rituals of degradation and punishment that attracted large crowds of onlookers.[46]

While Mexico's Holy Office was not as independent or as lethal as it had been, punishments for serious crimes against the faith were not light, and they followed pre-1700 patterns: floggings, exile, public shame, years of penal servitude, and fines.[47] Even with the three-judge panel's deference to regalist concerns, the late colonial Inquisition was still a tribunal of faith. It had not strayed far from its original focus on religious orthodoxy and moral offenses that violated Church teachings, such as bigamy, adultery, and deviant sexual habits. In fact, more cases of bigamy and false mystics were tried in the eighteenth century than earlier.[48] Amid these emphases, the trickle of priest impostors coming before the Inquisition in the sixteenth century continued two hundred years later. There were fewer trials overall in the eighteenth century, but the Inquisition generated more written records, including more open files of accusations and suspected offenses against the faith, thanks to the network of scores of district *comisarios* and their local *familiares* who were the Inquisition's eyes and ears throughout the viceroyalty. Their presence and the preliminary investigations they undertook continued to feed rumors and innuendo, which had always been a source of the Inquisition's influence. Being a *comisario* was still a prestigious position, often sought by leading local citizens.

The Inquisition's interest in Joseph Aguayo and Juan Atondo had little to do with threats they might pose to the crown, even though Atondo had been in the company of insurgents in 1813 and 1815. In spite of Atondo's insistence that he was a steadfast royalist, the prosecuting Inquisitor suspected otherwise, yet he did not investigate. Instead, he and his fellow judges were intensely interested in these two men because their crime was both a mortal sin and an intolerable affront to the integrity and prestige of the Holy Office and the Church. By repeatedly perverting a vital sacrament, their actions jeopardized the souls of those who had come to these impostors in good faith for confession and absolution. Perhaps equally important, the judges regarded these impostors' deeds as profoundly disrespectful of the court's dignity and good name. But it is important to remember that the interest was mutual. Atondo and especially Aguayo had good reason to prefer the uncertain mercies of the Inquisition to the jails and justice of the crown's district courts and the Audiencia's Real Sala del Crimen (the king's provincial high court sitting as a criminal tribunal). Nevertheless, while not sentenced to death, Aguayo and Atondo would pay dearly for pretending to be priests.

1 *Joseph Lucas Aguayo y Herrera, Escape Artist*

For an evasive man, Joseph Lucas Aguayo y Herrera has an unusually well documented life thanks to his having been charged in two Inquisition trials, implicated in a third, and investigated again twenty years later. There are more than six hundred pages of judicial records, witness testimony, short autobiographical statements, and various responses to charges against him to consider. Among other things, Aguayo reveals himself to be an accomplished liar, escape artist, and serial impersonator of priests. He had a confident way with words and a grifter's guile that was aided by his physical appearance. In all three descriptions of him for the tribunal in 1770, 1771, and 1773 by officials who would have considered themselves of Spanish descent, he was said to be of medium height and build, somewhat dark complected, with black hair, sparse facial hair, and black eyes. Except for his beak-like nose, the same could be said of many men of his time and place. These descriptions did not comment on his *casta*, or racial designation, but Aguayo himself claimed that he was of Old Christian, Spanish descent.[1] The less formal descriptions of Aguayo by five lay witnesses and a parish priest who encountered him dressed as a priest in Irapuato and León, Guanajuato, in 1768 were quite different. To them, he appeared to be an Indian—"un clérigo yndio," "padre yndito." Some said he had dark skin ("prieto"), others said he was "descolorido" (pallid or colorless). All said he was small— "short and slender in stature"—and "boyish" in appearance. One witness thought he was no more than seventeen or eighteen years old and certainly looked too young to be a priest. (Only ordained presbyters could be licensed to celebrate Mass and hear confessions. There was some debate over whether one had to be twenty-five years old or could be ordained during the twenty-fifth year, but either way, Aguayo was too young in 1769–70.) The common denominator in these official and unofficial descriptions was that he was smallish, young, and undistinguished in appearance. As one of the Irapuato witnesses put it, he had very little presence ("de muy poca presencia") and seemed harmless. Looks were deceiving.

Aguayo specialized in impersonation and theft (rather than robbery—there is little to suggest that he resorted to violence), often posing as an official in need of help. He rarely volunteered all the relevant details to his judicial interrogators, but he was arrested at least six times—probably more, given his passing admission of a "mala inclinación" (inclination toward delinquency) as a minor. All told, he spent about seventeen (he said twenty) of his first forty years in various jails or nominal penal servitude.[2] At least four times he escaped imprisonment, once he deserted military service, and several times he narrowly avoided arrest. From the time he was about fourteen, if he was not in custody, he was traveling without a set destination.

A Life on His Own and on the Move

"I left determined to make my way in life . . . for good or ill."

—JOSEPH AGUAYO[3]

Aguayo's childhood possibilities in the great mining center of Guanajuato during the mid-eighteenth-century boom traced a low arc. His baptism registration establishes that he was born on October 18, 1747, although he would confuse the issue in his second trial in 1773 by claiming he was twenty-three or twenty-four at that time. His father, an orphan who lived by sifting mine tailings for bits of silver ore (a *rescatador de piedras de plata*), was fourteen or fifteen when Aguayo was born, and his mother died young. His father remarried and had two more children, but Aguayo does not seem to have been included in family life. He mentioned a few other relatives, including two aunts, several cousins, an uncle in the priesthood, and at least one husband of an aunt, but apparently had nothing to do with any of them. At the age of ten or twelve he was sent to Querétaro for a rudimentary education, then to work on a ranch near San Miguel el Grande for a year. He returned to Guanajuato, where he studied briefly in a Jesuit school. Aguayo had very little to say about his teenage years except that he ran away from home several times and was on his own by age seventeen, traveling through central and western Mexico, mainly in Mexico City and the cities of Puebla, Guadalajara, Valladolid, Querétaro, Celaya, San Miguel el Grande, Pátzcuaro, and smaller towns in between.

In 1767, at age twenty, he was released from the Guanajuato jail and tried to return to his father's home.[4] In Aguayo's account, rather than welcoming him back, his father told his stepmother to lock him out without even a morsel of food. "I found myself cast into the shadow of poverty." Eight or nine days later he went back "to see if my father would at least leave me with some clothing."[5] But no, his father cursed him and sent him packing. He had been disowned by what there was in the way of kin.[6]

In his telling, Aguayo compressed the roughly three years until he was arrested in August 1770 for posing as a priest into a few inci-

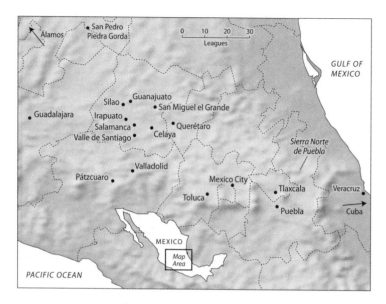

MAP 1. Joseph Aguayo's Mexico. Map by Bill Nelson.

dents of travel and travail, not far from his hometown, none of them flattering to him. His first stop after leaving Guanajuato was the town of Lagos on the edge of the Bajío region in Jalisco. There, "governed by my poverty,"[7] he stole a cloak, hat, and staff of office from the parish priest's nephew. The priest tracked Aguayo down in nearby León, Guanajuato, and had him arrested. He was released after returning the stolen goods, but "my straitened circumstances doubled because the jailer kept my cape and meager clothes."[8] Sometime in early 1768 he left León for Silao, where a kindly innkeeper gave him a piece of black woolen cloth. On the way to Irapuato, at a ranch that doubled as an inn, he presented himself as a priest and asked the innkeeper if he knew a tailor who could make a cassock for him from the cloth. The innkeeper took him on horseback to Irapuato and arranged for him to stay with a friend who lived next to a tailor. The innkeeper suggested that he collect alms from notables of the town, but Aguayo knew he would need a proper outfit in order to present himself as a priest worthy of respect. The tailor made him a basic cassock, but as soon as he went out to collect alms he noticed a priest in the street who might well have been the parish pastor, so he ducked into the church sacristy. A parishioner, mistaking him for a priest, asked if he would say Mass. He obliged and received a small stipend. He left the church and went on to Irapuato's hospital chapel, where he was again asked to celebrate Mass, this time receiving a stipend of four *reales*. At the urging of the pious family that opened their home to him, he confessed a sick woman.

Fearing he would be found out, he moved on to Salamanca and then to nearby Valle de Santiago, where he said his third Mass before making a detour to Apaseo, perhaps to evade pursuers or because he had reason to anticipate a warm reception from the local priest. He did not say. Instead he said that it was a Sunday and he meant only to attend Mass, but the assistant pastor there spotted him and invited him to go to the Hacienda de Jáuregui. There the assistant pastor said Mass, then told Aguayo to say another Mass and collect four *reales*, which he did, "opening the missal to the same places as the priest."[9] After Mass, they left together and on the road the priest gave him a cassock and pastor's manual, and loaned him vestments to use temporarily. Fearing the priest would realize he was an impostor, Aguayo made for Valladolid some twenty-seven leagues[10] south, by way of the predominantly Indian parishes of Acámbaro, Zinapécuaro, Indaparapeo, and Charo, perhaps on horseback or muleback now, which would give a boost to his official appearance as well as make long-distance travel easier. In Valladolid he said he celebrated his fifth Mass for a fee of four

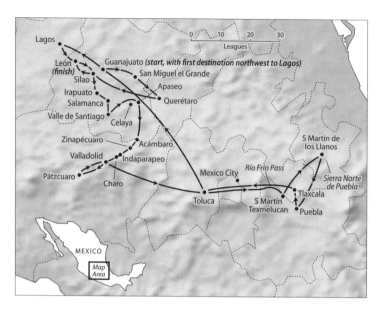

MAP 2. Main Stops in Joseph Aguayo's Travels, 1768–70. Map by Bill Nelson.

reales because of his "cresidas nesesidades" (growing needs) and the persistent requests of local people. From Valladolid he traveled to Pátzcuaro, then back to Valladolid and eventually on to Toluca, more than fifty leagues to the east, where he celebrated a sixth Mass for a stipend of one peso, with the permission of the Franciscan *padre guardián*, even though Aguayo did not present a license to do so.

Months slip by without comment in Aguayo's narrative. But he was on the move, appearing next in San Martín Texmelucan, located about forty leagues east of Toluca across the Río Frío pass, a fabled meeting place of highway robbers and vagabonds between the Iztaccíhuatl volcano and Mount Tlaloc from the Valley of Mexico into Tlaxcala. Wearing clerical garb again, he reached

Texmelucan in May in the company of two young men from Puebla he had met at Río Frío and introduced as his attendants. (They would later say that they were the servants of a priest in Puebla named Doctor Navarro, that they had only just met Aguayo, and that they did not know whether he was a priest or not.) Aguayo introduced himself to Don Juan Ignacio Lardizábal, the parish priest, as a fellow clergyman, a deacon from "tierra adentro"—the northern provinces of New Spain—and asked him for lodging. Unfortunately for Aguayo, Father Lardizábal was also the local ecclesiastical judge (*juez eclesiástico*) and agent of the Inquisition (*comisario*). He was suspicious, especially when Aguayo gave vague answers to questions about certain Church ceremonies. The priest wondered whether Aguayo wore clerical garb just to make his travels more comfortable ("para pasarlo mejor") or whether there was something more sinister in his impersonation. Suspecting that Aguayo would try to flee, Father Lardizábal had him shackled and locked in the sacristy. After two weeks there, Aguayo complained that he was gravely ill and persuaded the priest's lay assistant to remove the shackles. A night or two later, apparently with the tacit knowledge of the acting sacristan, Antonio Ribera (who went by the nickname Muégano, meaning "caramel candy"), Aguayo tied bedsheets together, lowered himself to the ground through the sacristy window, and fled, leaving Ribera with a pair of black pants, a shirt, and several silver reliquaries he had taken from the church.[11] In his haste Aguayo also left behind two horses, a saddle, more clothing, and an old copy of the Divine Office (the breviary, or book of prescribed prayers sanctifying each day), all of which the Inquisition later sold to cover court costs.

He mentioned being arrested in early March in San Martín de los Llanos, the mountains of northern Puebla (Sierra Norte de

Puebla), for presenting himself in clerical garb to the parish priest, but claimed he had not celebrated Mass or confessed anyone there. In June or July he was in the city of Puebla, again arrested for presenting himself as a priest and confessing two men who gave him four *reales* for a Mass. From there he moved on to Tlaxcala and then back to Toluca and Guanajuato. By September he was in jail in Querétaro, apparently for posing as an assayer of the royal mint and collecting a share of the silver he pretended to test and certify. There he made a declaration admitting to the arrests in Puebla and asking to be remanded to the jurisdiction of the Inquisition. No action was taken on his request, and nine months later, in July 1769, he was released after agreeing to military service in a new infantry regiment stationed at Querétaro. (The option of military service was offered more often to young men charged with nonviolent crimes during the eighteenth century. Military service by enlisted men had fallen from favor as a prestigious occupation since the seventeenth century, and the crown needed more boots on the ground, mainly for defense against foreign threats.) He deserted a few weeks later.

Perhaps overconfident in his talent as an impersonator and fugitive, Aguayo found himself in serious trouble in León in early October 1769. On October 10, the *alcalde mayor* of León, Licenciado don Martín Joachin de Andónaegui, reported that Aguayo had come to him the night before dressed as a priest and carrying a fine staff of office with a gold-plated cap stamped with the insignia of the Inquisition to complain that the innkeeper where he was staying had taken possession of his horse. Aguayo told him he was a priest and *comisario* of the Holy Office of the Inquisition on an important official errand and needed the *alcalde mayor*'s assistance in recovering the horse. Instead of going directly to the inn, Andónaegui consulted León's ecclesiastical judge. The judge had Aguayo arrested, recognizing him as having been arrested in León once before for theft and impersonating a priest.

From the León jail, Aguayo made a preliminary confession and asked that his case be remanded to the Inquisition in Mexico City. He identified himself as an *español* from Guanajuato, twenty-one years old, in training to be a surgeon. He said he had been on his way north to see a relative in San Pedro Piedra Gorda. Stopping in León, he lodged in the home of María de Herrero. When he returned there from an errand, he found his mare missing and was told that Herrero had taken it, so he went to complain to the *alcalde mayor*. He admitted telling the *alcalde mayor* he was on official Inquisition business. He also admitted that he had presented himself as a priest, and had stolen the staff of office and an old hat from a priest in Celaya, and a silver serving spoon and censer from the Chapel of the Holy Cross in Silao. He had had the censer melted down and sold the silver to an accountant in León. He also admitted that he had said three Masses in Guanajuato, but maintained that he had legitimately bought the horse in Marfil, a mining community outside the city of Guanajuato.

The next day the *alcalde mayor* summoned several local witnesses. The first was Ygnacio Herrera, eighteen, who had befriended Aguayo on the road from Silao. Aguayo had been wearing a ragged blue garment and clerical collar, and carrying his staff of office. He mentioned that he was a priest and *comisario* of the Inquisition, and had celebrated Mass in San Miguel el Grande two years before. Herrera arranged for Aguayo to spend the night at his mother's house. The next day Aguayo moved to a nearby hostel, where he told the owners that he had celebrated Masses in Guanajuato for a stipend of twenty pesos each. Herrera showed Aguayo where he could have his clothes washed and where he could sell the silver spoon, and introduced him to a blacksmith who would melt down an old silver saltcellar for him. Aguayo said he was selling these items to make ends meet while the official business he had come for was pending. That night the two of them went to a public *fandango*, where Aguayo was treated as a dignitary, occupying one of the principal seats of honor, wearing his clerical collar and carrying the staff of office.

Four other residents of León who had spoken to Aguayo came forward: the accountant who purchased the silver spoon, the blacksmith who had melted down the salt cellar, and María Manuela de Córdoba and her thirteen-year-old daughter, María Raphaela, of the household where Aguayo lodged the second night. The first two merely reported their transactions and said that Aguayo seemed to be a traveling priest, with his staff and black outfit. Aguayo apparently was more expansive in his conversation with the Córdoba women. When they invited him to stay for the upcoming feast of Todos Santos and assured him he could collect considerable fees, he replied that he could collect much more in his hometown of San Miguel el Grande—more in one day there than if he stayed here for the rest of the year. Twice he said he was a priest and everyone there took him at his word because of his self-assurance and clerical collar, staff, and cape. A witness from Irapuato came next, testifying to the two Masses Aguayo had celebrated there and the confession he had heard the previous year.

During further interrogation the next day, Aguayo said he had been dressing as a priest only for the past two weeks, as a disguise after deserting his regiment, and did not admit to any thefts other than the one in Lagos two years before. He did admit that he had boasted to the Córdobas about the fees and offerings he could collect in San Miguel and Guanajuato, but he claimed that that was to excuse himself from staying on in León. Asked where he had been or settled, what clothing he wore, and whether he had celebrated Masses and confessed penitents, he said he had been in Mexico City, Celaya, Querétaro, Toluca, Guanajuato, San Miguel el Grande, Salamanca, Silao, Irapuato, Acámbaro, Valle de Santiago, Zinapécuaro, Indaparapeo, Charo, Valladolid, Pátzcuaro, and throughout the sierra, but had not confessed anyone or celebrated Mass. But now he did admit to the Masses he had celebrated in Irapuato, Valle de Santiago, Apaseo, and Valladolid.

There was a question of overlapping jurisdictions—Aguayo had committed offenses against the laws of the crown as well as the Church—and the *alcalde mayor* continued to hold Aguayo in his jail until April of the next year, but the Inquisition eventually gained precedence and its dossier on Aguayo began to thicken with administrative actions, testimony, charges, and responses. In November 1769 the Inquisition commissioned testimony from two priests and four laymen of Irapuato and Valle de Santiago who had encountered Aguayo when he passed through town in 1768, when he had celebrated Mass and confessed a sick woman. All regarded him as a surprisingly young and diminutive Indian priest, but the chaplain of Valle de Santiago said he grew suspicious when his sacristan interrupted Aguayo's preparations to celebrate Mass by asking him to present his licenses. Aguayo said he would do so, but then engaged the sacristan in idle conversation to avoid the question of the licenses. Aguayo took his leave and the chaplain soon discovered he had gone back to his lodgings, so he sent the local notary there to bring Aguayo to the *alcalde mayor*.

But with great cunning, he [Aguayo] deceived the notary, suggesting that they go together to where he had left his papers, then on the way telling him that he had neither titles nor licenses because four months earlier they were suspended because he had wounded a soldier. Then who knows what threats he made, but he struck fear in the poor notary and made his escape from the valley. Now I have heard that he is saying Mass in La Magdalena, two leagues from here, a small community of pure Indians who will know no better than to receive him.[12]

More witnesses from León were called in March 1770, repeating the testimony they had given earlier.

On April 5 Aguayo was ordered removed to the Inquisition cells, and his belongings were seized. Soon thereafter, an armed escort assigned to move their shackled prisoner to the offices of the Inquisition in Mexico City began the journey. On May 4 the party reached the Valley of Mexico and stopped for the night at Tlalnepantla. Still shackled and guarded by six "indios," Aguayo somehow escaped before dawn. The Inquisition quickly ordered a manhunt, broadcasting a description of the fugitive that closely matched how the citizens of Irapuato had described him, as "small, skinny, pallid, and looking to be about seventeen or eighteen years old."[13] Aguayo was finally apprehended for good on July 6 in San Pedro Piedra Gorda, Zacatecas, more than one hundred leagues north of the Valley of Mexico. The *alcalde mayor* of León took Aguayo into custody and was reluctant to turn him over to the Inquisition's *comisario* because he had committed crimes against the state by posing as an official of the royal mint—a *juez comisionado de quintos*. Aguayo himself clearly preferred the Inquisition. As he put it in a letter received by the Inquisition in Mexico City on

August 22, "There are serious charges pending against me in this Holy Tribunal and I wish to confess my crimes and be reconciled to the Church once and for all."[14] With the approval of Viceroy Marqués de Croix, Aguayo was transferred to Inquisition custody on August 26. He was presented for inspection the next day, described as a bachelor, twenty-one or twenty-two years old, surgeon by profession, claiming the status of a Spaniard ("calidad español"), medium in stature, black hair, dark skin, sparse facial hair, black eyes, and the distinctive aquiline nose. Cutting a dapper figure, he wore a shirt of coarse cotton cloth, pants of semi-fine white linen topped with heavier trousers sporting a metal button, black wool stockings, cordovan shoes with gold-plated metal buckles, a cap made of Brittany cloth, and a blue and white kerchief at his throat, and carried a fine woolen shawl.

Aguayo spent nearly half a year in the Inquisition cells before his trial was completed. Since he was under twenty-five years old, he was entitled to representation by a court-appointed attorney, but the charges leveled by the *inquisidor fiscal*, José Gregorio Ortigoza (who went on to become bishop of Oaxaca from 1775 to 1791), were serious. He had impersonated a *comisario* of the Inquisition; impersonated a priest and repeatedly celebrated Mass and confessed penitents; collected stipends for these bogus services; stolen sacred things from individuals and churches; and twice escaped imprisonment ordered by officials of the Holy Office. Without admitting to celebrating more than six Masses or hearing more than a few confessions, and insisting that he had not served communion to any of the penitents, Aguayo apologized profusely for his vile behavior, but insisted that there was no heretical intent. Rather, those were the deeds of a morally weak, miserable sinner who wanted to be regarded as a priest.

In Ortigoza's judgment, Aguayo's behavior constituted "apostatized heresy from Our Holy Faith, or at the very least the suspicion of it being so, and contempt for the holy sacraments."[15] Ortigoza added the customary assurance that justice would be tempered with mercy: "If we were to apply the full extent of the laws, we would need to condemn him to great and grave punishment, but we wish to moderate the punishment with equity and mercy for several just reasons that move us."[16]

On Sunday, January 24, 1771, Aguayo's sentence was read after Mass in Mexico City's Church of Santo Domingo with the prisoner standing before the congregation, dressed in the conical hat of a penitent, insignias of guilt and repentance on his tunic, and carrying a lighted candle. The next day he was flogged two hundred times while being paraded through the city on a donkey, naked from the waist up, with a noose around his neck and wearing the conical hat, while the town crier broadcasted his crimes. He was sentenced to ten years' exile—forbidden to come within twenty leagues of Madrid, Mexico City, and all the sites of his crimes. The first five years of the sentence were to be spent in penal servitude without pay on the fortifications of Havana, Cuba. He was also to make a sacramental confession within two months, and again during the High Holy Days of Christ's Resurrection, the Epiphany, and Pentecost of the following year, and to pray the rosary every Saturday during that year as well. He was soon sent on the rope line of prisoners to Veracruz to await passage to Cuba.

Aguayo was in a world of trouble, but he was about to make things worse. In June 1772, after spending eight months laboring on the ramparts of the fortifications at Veracruz, he bribed a guard and escaped again, making his way on foot to Mexico City and north to his hometown of Guanajuato, ripe with opportunity for theft and deception, where he posed variously as a priest and a royal collector of Indian tribute. Along the way he succeeded in relieving several citizens of their money and stealing a horse and a priest's hat and cane. Arrested in Guanajuato three months later by the Inquisition's *comisario*, he spent the next five months in the local jail. In the Inquisition cells in 1773, we get another physical description and something of a character assessment of Aguayo. He again identified himself as an *español*, descended from Old Christians. He was literate and a bachelor, twenty-three or twenty-four years old, he said. (He was actually twenty-five or twenty-six, another of the half-truths he would tell under oath.) He again spoke of his father as an orphan and widower who lived by sifting through mine tailings for bits of silver ore. He had run away from home more than once by the time he was sixteen, and left for good at seventeen, moving from place to place, mostly to cities in central and western Mexico. The Inquisition's notary described him as medium in height and build, with dark skin, black hair and eyes, sparse facial hair, and aquiline nose. This time he was wearing a coarse woolen poncho, an old frock coat of blue cloth, cinnamon-colored pants of Castilian cloth, a shirt and cap of Brittany cloth, a black hat, white wool stockings, and buttoned shoes.

During his extended stay in the Guanajuato jail in 1772, Aguayo met a fellow prisoner, Augustín Solano, who became a collaborator and mentor of sorts. Solano was a rougher character, ten years older than Aguayo, a cunning, if deluded, hedonist and felon who would later appeal for leniency from the Inquisition with a show of his feigned "rusticity and limited abilities" ("rudeza y corta capacidad"). He told fellow prisoners in the Guanajuato jail that he had an intimate association with the Devil, who appeared to him as a terrifying man or a snake and gave him special powers. Aguayo and other prisoners reported that Solano claimed he had made a formal pact with the Devil and could now do as he pleased: bullets aimed at him missed their target; he could get the women he wanted and also spy on them from many leagues away; and he rode the finest horses because under him old nags became spirited stallions. He told Aguayo the Devil had even made it possible for him to break out of prison in Mexico City recently and would do so again for both of them if they honored the Devil by eating Rosa María (cannabis) while reciting the Apostles' Creed and Marian hymns on Fridays for visions and auguries, defacing images of Christ and the Virgin in the prison chapel, and renouncing God. Solano declared that the Devil would provide for him in the here and now, as God was powerless to do, and that through the Devil's patronage he was more powerful than God or the Virgin. God was just a piece of old wood, and Rosa María was more effective than the Blessed Mary because it spoke and often appeared in the form of a woman.

Perhaps crossing his fingers, Aguayo became the sorcerer's apprentice.[17] He recited the prayers Solano prescribed, blasphemed, and took the Rosa María as directed, although he said he did not see a woman, only some dark figures that appeared to be men, and they did not speak. Solano told him that in order to enjoy the full effect and escape from jail, he needed to renounce God, damage statues of the Mater Dolorosa and Christ in the prison chapel, mutilate religious medals and prints, take communion four times without swallowing the consecrated wafers, hide the wafers along with one Solano had, and offer them to the Devil. Aguayo testified that they did deface some images, but that he had not tried to get the consecrated wafers because it was impossible to do so without being observed. He did fast one Friday, as Solano instructed, and offered this sacrifice to Rosa María with various credos and salves, and repeated Solano's curses.

When Aguayo and Solano were denounced for their desecrations and heresy at the beginning of January 1773, theirs appeared to be a case of magical thinking that fizzled. But if we can believe what they professed to the Inquisition later that year, it was all a ruse they hatched to get themselves transferred from the Guanajuato jail to the Inquisition's jurisdiction; Solano said he had heard that this Holy Tribunal had great power to release him from the punishment his earlier escape called for.[18] Their agreement ("convenio," as Solano called it) was for Aguayo to spread the word among fellow prisoners that they were plotting to escape by means of this "diabolical witchcraft" and then go through the motions of appealing to the Devil "even though, in truth, it was all lies and falsehoods . . . meant to get themselves sent to this tribunal."[19] If this was the plan, it worked. Solano was moved to the Inquisition cells first, then Aguayo some weeks later. The trip from Guanajuato was no cakewalk. It took about six weeks, as Aguayo was passed in shackles from one local jail to the next. At the last stop before reaching Mexico City, he was mounted on a pack mule and given two hundred lashes as his escort paraded him through the streets of the city.

Lodged in separate cells, Aguayo and Solano exchanged brief messages scribbled on walls and the bottoms of serving bowls. Solano's first message was, "Father, I am in number 16. What have you told them?"[20] Solano urged Aguayo to deny all their diabolical acts and promises and repeated that, if they did so, the Devil would protect them. But they soon turned against each other. Aguayo began to tell the tribunal a different story: he himself had not made a pact with the Devil, but Solano's witchcraft was real. He had played along out of desperation in order to learn from Solano the secret of how to escape. He felt intimidated by the more imposing, older man and followed his instructions. He swore that Solano truly had made a pact with the Devil, as his prison mates in Guanajuato had testified. Aguayo eventually admitted that he had stolen four consecrated Hosts at Solano's request and supplied the religious prints Solano sacrilegiously put in his shoes and used as cigarette wrappers.

For his part, Solano testified that he, too, had acted out of desperation in the Guanajuato jail—but that it was all a ruse. There was no pact with the Devil. He had learned the superstitious lore and obtained the Rosa María from other prisoners there, and had passed on his knowledge to the equally desperate Aguayo. Now, he said, Aguayo was lying: Aguayo himself was the instigator of all this trouble, and had written all the notes Solano had with him in the Inquisition cells about faking their devotions to the Devil. (Aguayo would reply that Solano dictated the words in those notes.) Under interrogation, Solano deflected questions about his past experience with witchcraft and was less than forthcoming when questioned about some of his actions in the Guanajuato jail, saying that he could not remember what was said or done. He did admit he had had an illicit affair with a witch in Mexico City called La Pantera (The Panther) and had put prints of Our Lady of Dolores in his shoes, but denied walking in them.

Sensing that Aguayo was in more serious trouble, Solano told the Inquisitors an airbrushed tale about being an upstanding but ignorant bumpkin who had fallen prey to liquor, glossing over his years of witchcraft, violent crimes, and imprisonment. Now thirty-four, he said he had lived with his parents in Cadereyta until he was ten or twelve years old. He spent two years apprenticed to a silversmith in Mexico City, then returned to his hometown, working in his aunt's house as a silversmith. He had fulfilled the Easter Duty of confession and communion and usually attended Mass until about six years ago, when his drinking landed him in jail and penal servitude. (In colonial practice, drunkenness alone would not have resulted in a lengthy sentence. Aguayo claimed Solano had committed armed robberies and murder in Cadereyta.) After eleven months he escaped and went into hiding for about two years in the Cadereyta area. He then went to Pachuca and Mexico City, where he gave himself up to the Inquisition for witchcraft. After he was pardoned he went to work briefly in the Guanajuato mines and was arrested for his escape from prison and sent to the Guanajuato jail, where he met Aguayo.

Curiously, the Inquisitors skimmed over the evidence in Solano's dossier that he had appeared before the tribunal in 1767 and admitted to practicing witchcraft. At that time, Solano had shrewdly come forward "spontaneously" rather than waiting for the Inquisition to catch up with him. He confessed he had been a follower of Manuel Zervantes, an Indian sorcerer from San Luis de la Paz, who promised him that through the black arts everything would go well with him: he would be granted his wish to become a fine horseman, bullfighter, and warrior. Solano admitted that he had once supplied Zervantes with three consecrated Hosts when told they were needed to bargain with the Devil for Solano's release from prison. Zervantes allegedly convinced Solano that he would be granted other wishes if he made certain potions. According to Solano, Zervantes had made a pact with the Devil, but he himself was only following instructions; only after making a full, sacramental confession and being reprimanded by his confessor had he come to understand the gravity of his acts.

Emphasizing his "rusticidad" in those 1767 proceedings, Solano appealed for the Inquisition's mercy. The Inquisitors tried to probe the murky waters of motive for Solano's abominable superstitions and sacrileges. Did he believe that the Devil was more powerful than Christ? No, Solano responded. Everything he had said against God and the True Faith "was purely with his mouth, not with his heart."[21] Several witnesses testified that Solano had an explicit pact with the Devil, and the Inquisitors found Solano's transgressions to be abominable, but they were swayed by his voluntary confession and "rustic" character. They absolved him under caution, with a prescription for "medicinal penances" ("penitencias medicinales")—to frequent the sacraments and do whatever else his confessor "considered opportune" ("que considere oportuno")—and gave him a stern warning that serious consequences awaited if he repeated his offenses against the True Faith.

While there is no record of the sentence in Solano's 1773 case file, the *inquisidor fiscal* certainly was more sympathetic to him and his story than to Aguayo. While he considered Solano "guilty of being a vehement apostate heretic and suspected notorious forger," the author of a long list of crimes and evil deeds that were "incompatible with a firm and constant faith in Church doctrine,"[22] those deeds were, in the end, merely "external" ones ("actos exteriores"). Aguayo's flouting of the Inquisition's authority by his flight from Veracruz, his claim to be a *comisario* of the Holy Office, and his return to impersonating a priest were more serious matters. That was clear from the whipping Aguayo endured on the way into the city even before the tribunal reviewed his case. Whatever the truth in his claims about Solano's many sins, Aguayo had been a willing accomplice in what appeared to be witchcraft.

In their 1773 verdict, the Inquisitors judged Aguayo to be more than the naive delinquent he claimed to be. Prosecuting Inquisitor Ortigoza knew Aguayo's record only too well, having presided over his first trial. Aguayo was, he judged, a threat to the faith and good order. He had mocked the tribunal's original sentence by taking flight from Veracruz, again committed his "enormous" offense of impersonating a priest, and committed other acts against the True Faith, including the sacrileges with Solano. He was a depraved apostate and suspected minion of Satan, not just a petty villain. The Inquisition essentially reimposed the original sentence, adding three years to the term of penal servitude. Aguayo had already been given another two hundred lashes. Now he was sentenced to ten years' exile and eight years' hard labor in coastal fortifications far from the scenes of his crimes. He was again subjected to the public humiliation of an *auto de fe* in the great Dominican church and streets of Mexico City, and a course of spiritual exercises.

In January 1775, after a few months in Veracruz, Aguayo was sent to Cuba to serve out the sentence of exile and penal labor. He remained in Cuba for fourteen years in all, until early 1789. For where he was and what he did during that time we have mainly Aguayo's word, but a few damning admissions give a ring of truth, or at least an echo of it, to his testimony about those years. He said he first was put to work in Havana's shipyards for five months, then served as scribe aboard a royal ship guarding the island's coast until early 1777, when he was left for dead at Puerto de Casilda on the southern coast of central Cuba after the ship caught fire during an attack by British warships. He escaped from the city of Trinidad's hospital and spent some months as a fugitive, moving from place to place on the island. He was arrested in October 1777 and sentenced to ten years' service without pay at a fortress near Santiago. (It would come out later, from another source, that he was arrested for theft.) At that time, he said, he changed his name to José Montero to hide the fact that he had deserted and not yet completed the original sentence. He did not specify the "various jobs" he did at Santiago, but my guess is that he used his literacy and way with words to earn light duty that saved him from the backbreaking labor and early death of most fellow prisoners.

After his release from the Santiago fortress ten months early, in May 1786, Aguayo eventually found passage to Veracruz in 1789, and from there traveled to Puebla, where he entered a local hospital for more than a month with fever and chills. He made his way to Mexico City, where he again fell ill and recuperated in a charity hospital. By late March he left on foot for Guanajuato. It was slow going. He was still not well and had no means of support other than begging. Briefly sighted in Guanajuato in late April, Aguayo was well remembered by the local *comisario* and, when he returned in July, was arrested on suspicion of escaping from Cuba before his sentence was up. The *comisario* reported that the documentation Aguayo presented looked suspicious. It amounted to two blank certificates of release and a third one crudely filled out in the name of "José Montero." Aguayo also carried a letter with a crude signature authorizing his early release, ostensibly from the governor of Santiago, which served him as a kind of passport, now sprinkled with signatures of officials in the larger towns he passed through from Veracruz on the way to Guanajuato.

The lead Inquisitor agreed with the *comisario* that Aguayo could well be lying and should be detained until officials in Veracruz and Cuba reported on when, and under what circumstances, he had left their jurisdictions. The intendant of the city and province of Veracruz quickly confirmed that Aguayo had been shipped to Cuba a few months after he began serving his sentence there. The response from officials in Cuba was slow in coming, and in October 1789 Aguayo appealed to the Inquisition "with all due humility, resignation, and utter veneration,"[23] as he put it, noting that he had been held in the Guanajuato jail for six months, on top of what he called the twenty years of grueling confinement he had already endured, "suffering all sorts of torments that the most searching intelligence can hardly imagine,"[24] which drained away "the cream of my flourishing youth" ("lo más lúcido de mi florida juventud"). He described himself as a broken and sick man, a miserable sinner. He explained again that the documents for his release in Cuba were in the name of José Montero because that was the alias he adopted when he was incarcerated the second time in Cuba. The Inquisitors relented and released him on condition that he "behave properly" and check in with Guanajuato's *comisario* once a week. Six months later the *comisario* reported that Aguayo had complied. Aguayo then asked for, and received, permission to move north to the burgeoning mining town of Álamos, Sonora. A few months later, a report arrived from Cuba largely confirming his account of his early release from the fortress at Santiago.

Aguayo Presents Himself: Reading His Actions and Words

". . . leaving nothing behind but my shadow"

—FRANCISCO DE QUEVEDO'S *PÍCARO*, PABLOS, *EL BUSCÓN*[25]

It is no surprise that Aguayo was contrite in the presence of the Inquisition, as he explained who he was, what he had done, and why. But his emphasis shifted from the first trial to the second, and again in his third encounter with the tribunal in 1789. During the first trial beginning in 1769 he touched familiar bases of regret and justification. He declared himself "flustered and confused" in the presence of this Holy Tribunal, remorseful for "my many and enormous crimes . . . the errors and evil deeds my meager self has committed . . . [and the] the extremely serious nature of my errors."[26] He said he was disgusted by his failure to resist temptation, but had had no malicious intent. His youth, lack of experience, and unpolished ways were partly to blame, but it was especially his poverty— "cresidas necesidades"—and his father's mistreatment that drove him into the darkness.[27]

In the second trial, Aguayo knew he was in even deeper trouble and dispensed with the sociological explanation of poverty and family. He organized his presentation of self to the tribunal around a plea for mercy, stressing that he was unburdening his conscience fully this time, and that he had been a great sinner, "a bad Christian who abused the dogmas of the Faith"[28] and authored very great crimes. He repented his crimes "with all my heart" ("con todo mi corazón") and promised to mend his ways in the future. "God well knows the tears of the sorrowful Mary [Dolores] I have shed for my sins here in my solitude." Now "with all my soul, obedient and ready to receive . . . the penitence that this Holy Tribunal may impose, I ask that it be with great charity."[29]

When he was arrested again in Guanajuato in 1789 on suspicion of escaping Cuba before completing his sentence, he appealed to the judges' benevolence with "the appropriate humility, resignation, and utter veneration owed to the notorious charity that this Holy Tribunal exhibits." He assured them that he was among "the true penitents who beg for mercy with all my heart."[30]

Aguayo's repertoire of presentations to the Inquisition responded to his changing circumstances and experiences, and they reflected his opportunism, acting in ways he judged best suited to the moment. Patterns in his testimony over the years, and his actions as he wrote about them and as witnesses described them, sometimes can take us behind the curtain, but we, as well as his eighteenth-century audience, are usually left in doubt about what he valued, what resentments he harbored, how he saw himself in the world, and what moved him to act as he did. He emphasized that he was from Spanish, Old Christian stock, but little in his life on the loose suggests that he cared much about honor or shame, as literary *pícaros* often did. His childhood was precarious, with a young, widowed father of modest means, barely able to sign his name, whose second wife had no patience for this son from a first marriage. Aguayo admitted to his "evil inclinations" ("mala inclinación") in boyhood and running away from home repeatedly as a teenager, but he glided over months and years of his personal history unless the tribunal pressed him for details, as it did only about his impersonations, escapes, apostasy in Solano's company, and the date of his birth. How did he get by during his absences in boyhood and for the three or four years between the time he left home for good and his arrest for impersonating a priest? Had theft and swindles already become his way of life? How many times was he arrested during those years? What about the three years in Cuba after he was released from presidio service?

Aguayo was a master of the partial truth. He understated his age when it suited him and exaggerated the length of time he spent in custody. He readily admitted to several thefts, celebrating six Masses, hearing some confessions, and one fleeting impersonation of a priest at a home in Jalapa after he escaped from Veracruz, but the convenient gaps in his chronological narrative led the *inquisidor fiscal* to conclude that he must have committed far more thefts, swindles, and impersonations than he admitted to. And his more damning admissions were strategic. He had to admit that he had deserted in Cuba in order to explain the alias he used on his release papers, one of which looked like it had been filled out by an amateur, perhaps Aguayo himself. He did not say why he had eventually been rearrested in Cuba and sentenced to ten more years of penal servitude. Was it only for the theft or thefts that Cuban officials found in their registers in 1789?

Apparently Aguayo was less circumspect and even a bit cocky in his small-town destinations among ordinary people—posing authoritatively as a priest or royal official, spinning stories of his travels, priestly doings, and income from Masses, trading more in outright lies. The silver tongue he displayed in his travels can occasionally be glimpsed in the written record, as when he appealed for mercy to the Inquisition in 1789 while gesturing to the hardships he had endured.[31] More than once he charmed innocent citizens out of their possessions with an urgent appeal to official needs. His Masses seemed authentic to his audience because he had paid attention to detail. He said that when he had assisted at Mass as a boy, he had memorized the parts of the Mass, and for the prayers and other spoken parts he "used a low voice so that those who attended would not recognize his ignorance."[32] Before celebrating Mass at the Hacienda de Jáuregui near Irapuato, he was careful to notice which pages of the missal his companion priest used, and then opened it to those pages when it was his turn.[33] But the scheme he hatched with Solano in the Guanajuato jail and carried to the cells of the Inquisition in 1772–73 was a serious stumble that led the *inquisidor fiscal* to regard his entire account as a pack of lies.

Aguayo described himself as a loner, cast adrift to make his way in the world, and it appears that he was. He insisted that up to the time of his first arrest in 1768 he had been on his own for some years. When he escaped from prison in Tlalnepantla and

Texmelucan in 1769 and Veracruz in 1772 he acted alone, he said, and usually traveled by himself until he was run to ground a few months later. Was he an empty heart and soul, self-absorbed and without apparent bonds of affection or attachment to place? He returned to the Guanajuato area several times, but no wife is mentioned in the record, nor any friendships except of convenience, and those quickly abandoned.[34] Despite years of imprisonment and penal servitude in Guanajuato, Cuba, Mexico City, and local jails in central Mexico, there is no indication that he became part of a criminal underworld.[35] The Inquisition considered him a rebel, a charge he repeatedly denied, with good reason—he had no cause other than his personal desires, and no lasting alliances. The lesson he took from his youthful experiences and betrayals, reinforced by the Solano episode, was to trust no one. People did him a good turn here and there, but he mentioned them only in passing, without gratitude or a sense of obligation. The Good Samaritan was not his model.

Inquisitors Take the Measure of Joseph Aguayo

"An escaped criminal and backslider"[36]

During the trial in 1770, Inquisidor Fiscal Ortigoza acknowledged Aguayo's talents—his literacy, his way with words and commendable knowledge of basic Church doctrine—but was convinced of the seriousness of the young man's offenses and the likelihood that this "mischievous, depraved character and utterly boundless liar" ("reo de ingenio travieso, de una continua estragada y embustero de inclinación") had committed more crimes and celebrated more Masses than the six he acknowledged. In short, Aguayo was judged a vile heretic. Except for a gnomic line in the 1770 verdict and a weak qualifier in the prosecutor's summary, the judges were not inclined to probe the web of misleading statements, selective candor, and extenuating circumstances Aguayo had presented to them and to the wider world. In all three trials, including the trial of Solano, the *inquisidor fiscal* described Aguayo's culpability in stark terms. In 1770 he wrote that Aguayo had

> forgotten his Christian obligations and vows, to the serious detriment and ruin of his soul . . . and set aside a holy fear of God and abandoned all respect and veneration for the righteousness and justice of this Holy Tribunal and the sacred determinations of the Church, abandoning its pure and holy bosom for the detestable, impure, and abominable ways of the Lutheran heretics. . . . He is an apostatizing heretic from Our Holy Catholic faith, or at least suspected of being so, who despises the Holy Sacraments and the jurisdiction of the keys of the Church, a scandalous perjurer who is used to committing many other more and less serious crimes within the purview of this Holy Office.[37]

Ortigoza declared that Aguayo deserved "grandes y graves penas" (great and grave punishment). But ecclesiastical judges were, in principle, expected to temper justice with mercy.[38] Aguayo's 1770 Inquisitors merely declared that they had reasons to mete out a "merciful" sentence. Beyond Aguayo's relative youth, just what those reasons were, we are left to wonder.

Unfortunately for Aguayo, Inquisitor Fiscal Ortigoza was still the prosecuting judge for the second trial in 1773. Ortigoza found these new crimes no less serious: violating his sentence by escaping from custody in Veracruz; impersonating a priest yet again; and the scandalous sacrileges and flirtation with diabolism he plotted with Solano. Ortigoza was in no hurry to complete the formalities of this second investigation and trial, but the verdict was a foregone conclusion since Aguayo had already received two hundred lashes on his way to the Inquisition cells, and this time there was no mention of reasons or considerations that might warrant the tribunal's indulgence. Hoping to gain the judges' sympathy or at least the services of a defense attorney, Aguayo tried to fudge his age, saying that he was twenty-three or twenty-four years old, but this time Ortigoza would have none of it. He ordered a search for Aguayo's baptism record and determined that the accused had already passed the threshold age of twenty-five for free legal representation. Aguayo was, he concluded, a threat to the faith and good order. He had committed "enormous" offenses against the True Faith, and was a truly depraved apostate.

It is somewhat surprising, then, that the sentence in 1773 was not much different from the one issued in the first trial, adding three years to the original five years of penal servitude. The perennial prospect of forgiveness and the possibility of redemption played a part, at least rhetorically, but by this time the Inquisition's power to impose harsher punishments was on the wane. Aguayo was threatened with torture in an effort to extract a full confession, but it was not applied. The *quemadero* (execution platform) in front of the convent of San Diego facing the Alameda park, where burnings at the stake had been carried out, was left in place until 1771, but the Inquisition had delivered no one to royal authorities for execution in more than seventy years. The 1771 verdict was not a failure of nerve on the Inquisition's part or an expression of ambivalence about Aguayo's crimes. It was a nod to the political realities of the time, and perhaps mercy. Neither sentence was light. Many who were flogged severely and sent to presidio service in the tropics did not return; Aguayo at least had a chance at life and redemption, as the tribunal evidently intended. But the deep stain of suspicion that marked Aguayo in the Inquisition's estimation had not faded when he returned to Guanajuato in 1789. Even after a seventeen-year absence, the Inquisition's *comisario* there remembered him and moved quickly to inform the tribunal in Mexico City of his presence. How could Aguayo have survived all those years of hard labor in the tropics? The Inquisitors were also suspicious. Only after another year of detention and spiritual exercises was he allowed to leave Guanajuato. By default, Aguayo would never be trusted by authorities after the first trial.

By all accounts, Aguayo was no one's follower and had no following, yet the Inquisition and its agents repeatedly went to considerable trouble and expense to pursue him. What did the Inquisitors see in this marginal character that prompted so much attention? Of course, pretending to carry out the sacramental duties of a priest was a deadly serious matter, imperiling souls and the spiritual bond between Christians and their God. But most cases of impersonation of priests since the sixteenth century had been dispatched quickly, without much probing and review. Aguayo's occasional impersonation of royal officials was a serious matter, too, but beyond the Inquisitors' purview. Aguayo's repeated escapes and recidivism go far to account for why he would have been seen as a more serious threat, but another long inquisitorial investigation and trial in the late 1570s—soon after the Holy Office was officially established in Mexico City—suggests an equally important reason. That case, a local affair involving slander in Tecamachalco, Puebla, revolved around an unpleasant man who bragged about having illicit sex with local married women. One night he was mocked in an anonymous display on the facade of the parish church of a dummy with two faces and two mouths, wearing a *sanbenito* (the scapular-like penitential bib worn by those judged to be heretics by the Inquisition). The Inquisition's interest in this affair was less in the possible heresy or Jewish identity of the target than in what the judges took to be his attackers' disrespect for the Inquisition itself and the symbols of its authority. The scandalous, mocking misuse of a *sanbenito* was what mattered most.[39] Aguayo's trials came at another delicate time, when the Inquisition's authority was in decline. The *inquisidor fiscal* in the early 1770s was especially concerned that Aguayo had posed as a *comisario* of the Inquisition, and had implicitly ridiculed the tribunal and subverted its authority and prestige by evading his court-ordered punishment, continuing to impersonate a priest, and pretending to celebrate Mass and confess penitents. The Inquisitors regarded Aguayo as a heretic, however contrite he claimed to be, but equally egregious was his disrespect for the authority and dignity of the tribunal.

Conclusion

"What I tell you is either truth or lies."

—MATEO ALEMÁN'S LITERARY *PÍCARO*,
GUZMÁN DE ALFARACHE[40]

Joseph Aguayo's show of contrition before the Inquisition, the selective silences he crafted there about his wayward life, and the judges' early hopes for his eventual redemption shaped his dossier into complementary stories of sin, confession, atonement, and redemption. But there is more to Aguayo than this duet. In person and on paper, he was an elusive character. When can he be taken at his word?

Aguayo operated on the fringes of society from childhood, as much by choice as from necessity. He was a risk-taker and an escape artist, a serial thief and a grifter, but not a thug. He was a quick study—a fluent writer and speaker even though his formal education was limited. Gaining the trust of ordinary people was his particular gift; he would say enough to persuade, but usually not so much as to arouse immediate suspicion. A performer who profited from the inability of others to see beneath his slight physique, cassock, and cane, he had the audacity to present himself to the *alcalde mayor* of Irapuato as a *comisario* of the Inquisition to complain about being robbed. And he was a survivor. In a time and place where the life expectancy of a fifteen-year-old male was another twenty years, he somehow managed to live into his forties, if not beyond, in spite of four hundred lashes, more than fifteen years of confinement, and many years on the move.[41]

What moved him to impersonate officials and choose small-time crime as a way of life, from young adulthood onward? Was it an inherent disposition—the self-ascribed "mala inclinación"—he had exhibited since childhood? Or, as he claimed in his first trial, did poverty and his father's rejection force him into theft and fraud just to scrape by? Or was it mainly the "rudeza" (lack of sophistication), youth, and inexperience of a miserable sinner, as he claimed in the trials? What can be said with some confidence is that the impersonations gratified Aguayo's desire for status, and suited his abilities as a literate performer more or less versed in the liturgy of the Church. Given his slight physique, he couldn't very well have gone in for violence. When asked to describe himself for the court he insisted he was an *español* and Old Christian. Like others who made this claim, he considered himself worthy of something better than manual labor.[42] And when he identified an occupation for the record, it was apprentice surgeon or practicing surgeon rather than the more accurate but lower-status barber or apprentice barber-surgeon. Above all, the cachet of being an official, especially a priest, appealed to him. It was gratifying as well as remunerative. Perhaps simply getting away with the deception was the main attraction. It is not hard to imagine him in his cassock occupying the seat of honor at the community *fandango* in León. The cassock and staff of authority also were his way into the polite company and hospitality of "fellow" priests or pious laymen at the end of a day's travels.

Posing as a priest was risky, especially if he celebrated Mass and heard confessions. Aguayo did not linger long after he did so. He was a confident performer at the altar, but the main reason he succeeded in the deception may be that people were thirsty for his services and felt that when they helped him, they were doing good work in the eyes of God. Consider the testimony of Joseph Bentura Gallardo, a thirty-year-old *mulato* bachelor from Irapuato. He met Aguayo on the road to Irapuato and found him unimpressive—"a little Indian dressed as a clergyman"—but "moved by compassion," he lifted Aguayo onto his horse, took him to town, put him up for a few days, and attended the Mass he celebrated in the Franciscan convent. He did all this "with pleasure in order to do a heroic act of charity; that is, to revere . . . the priests, especially poor ones, and so he looked for ways to give him what little he had."[43]

Setting Aguayo's command of doctrine and liturgy alongside his repeated sacrileges, it seems fair to wonder how he thought of himself as a Christian. He dutifully completed the spiritual exercises prescribed in his sentences, but could he have said or done otherwise while in the custody of the Inquisition? On the other hand, there were limits to his sacrileges. He explained to the Inquisitors that he had refrained from serving communion to the penitents he confessed because he knew that would be a great sin, and he claimed to be an ardent devotee of Our Lady of Sorrows and San Juan Nepomuceno (who was martyred for refusing to divulge the secrets of the confessional). He also carried a worn copy of the breviary for praying the Liturgy of the Hours. But perhaps that was more a stage prop than a text that actually punctuated his days with prayers to order his spiritual life?

The moral of Joseph Aguayo's life story for the parties involved, if there is one, is not clear. Even after his first escape and retrial on yet more serious charges, the Inquisitors still envisioned for him a trajectory of just punishment, absolution, and redemption. But when Aguayo finally returned from Cuba in 1789, in his forties, he seemed to be an utterly broken, spectral figure, presenting the Inquisitors with a less uplifting story of a misspent life and the bitter fruit of regret. Aguayo seemed sadder and wiser as he appealed for mercy, speaking of his "poor and miserable flesh exposed to public shame so that today I amount to a true symbol of compassion and misery worthy of the most gentle consideration."[44]

But this is not quite the end of the paper trail, or of Aguayo's surprises for readers expecting a thundering denouement or final redemption. There is one more document in his Inquisition files, and it suggests he had not mellowed with age, or with spiritual medicine. It is a notice from the office of the archbishop of Mexico from 1792, three years after the Inquisitors let Aguayo limp off to Álamos. It informed the Inquisition that Aguayo was alive and in prison again near Guanajuato for posing as a priest, among other misdeeds, with an irate *tintorero* (dyer) he had deceived in hot pursuit. Should he be remanded to the Inquisition, asked the archbishop's attorney? No, was the reply. The Inquisitors had seen enough of Joseph Aguayo.

2 *Juan Atondo's Vagrant Heart*

Juan Atondo had long imagined joining the priesthood, but his public impersonation of a priest lasted only a few months in 1815, when he was thirty-two years old. The impersonation was of a piece with his biography up to then—a dizzying succession of commitments made and broken, of arrivals and sudden departures. Atondo spoke and wrote of his actions, intentions, and feelings at unusual length during the three years or so he was in the Inquisition's custody, from October 1815 to late 1818. His voice is heard in interrogations, responses to formal charges, and witness testimony, but he speaks at greatest length in a rambling confession—thirty pages of script—that he wrote out unbidden. The confession is sprinkled with scattered details (such as where and when he had breakfast), loose ends (Did he ever pay off his debts? How did the supposedly chaste relationship with a woman in Orizaba end?), digressions (into his taste in clothes and method of confession), doubtful boasts, shamefaced admissions, and groveling apologies. The Inquisitors were less than captivated by his billowing mea culpa, but Atondo's rhetorical excesses are a gift for readers hoping to know more about him than the Inquisitors' depiction of a sly, obsequious apostate and contemptible liar.[1]

Aspirations and Transgressions

Here, briefly, is the turbulent course of Atondo's life, as he and others told it. Although he was often vague about year dates—yet surprisingly precise about months and days of the week—he was likely born in 1783, in Mexico City. He said his ancestors were Old Christian Spaniards in both lines, and he used the honorifics *don* and *doña* for his parents to suggest that his was a respectable family, even modestly distinguished. Atondo mentioned two uncles and a brother, about whom he said nothing except that he did not know the latter's surname or lineage, suggesting that he had a different father, but he may well have had a larger extended family in the capital city, since he later referred to the husband of an aunt whom he once asked for help. In any event, he wrote that all his relatives had disowned him by 1809 or 1810, fed up with his string of lies, broken promises, and other misdeeds.[2]

His widowed mother somehow paid for his early education from her meager means, but, he lamented, he was unable to continue his studies beyond the age of sixteen or so, when, with his "heart aflame with the love of God and Religion," he made a first attempt at becoming a Dieguino (Discalced Franciscan) novice.[3] He did not say why he sought membership in this austere branch of the Franciscans, but the fact that one of his uncles was a Dieguino may be the main reason. In any case, he did not last long there, owing, he said, to an illness he thought might be scurvy. The next year he failed twice more to restart the Dieguino vocation, again because of some unspecified illness.

At seventeen he was at loose ends, unhappily apprenticed to a tailor and entangled with a pregnant woman who claimed he was the father. Atondo insisted it wasn't so, that they had never engaged in sexual intercourse, but his mother told him firmly that he had two choices: marry the woman or enlist in the military and leave for "China." Instead, he joined the regiment of dragoons (light cavalry) in Mexico City and assured readers that his good conduct earned him the favor of his sergeant and colonel, who noticed his religious ardor and encouraged his studies. The colonel even gave him a copy of the famous Castilian grammar that Antonio de Nebrija presented to Queen Isabella in 1492, which remained a classroom primer three centuries later. The next year, perhaps it was 1801 or 1802, his regiment moved to the town of Orizaba, about thirty leagues east of Puebla on one of the two main routes to Veracruz. The regimental chaplain encouraged his desire for a deeper religious commitment, so he deserted his unit and took refuge in the recently established local Franciscan missionary college and convent, hoping to join this community of several dozen friars.[4] At first, he claimed he was an apostate from the Dieguinos in Mexico City, so that the guardian of the convent would arrest him rather than send him back to his unit. When it was discovered that Atondo had left the Dieguino convent for medical reasons rather than having apostatized, he was returned to the barracks, to the scorn and abuse of the soldiers. However, seeing "my ardent desire" ("mi ardiente deseo"), the Franciscans at Orizaba eventually allowed him to return to the convent after they paid for two recruits to take his place in the regiment.

He joined the convent community as a *donado*, or servant allowed to wear the Franciscan habit. He said he stayed there a long time ("mucho tiempo"). It may have been three years, perhaps a little longer. He claimed that his hard work, including caring for a deranged friar, was recognized, and that he was eventually allowed to profess and enter the novitiate. But Franciscan wit-

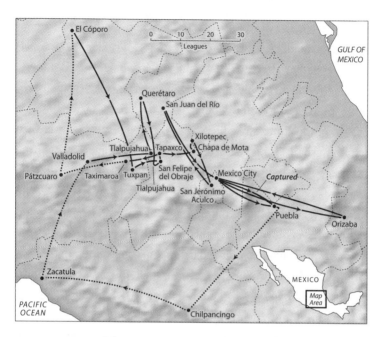

MAP 3. Juan Atondo's Travels, 1802–15. Map by Bill Nelson.

nesses later testified that he had not professed, and at the end of his trial Atondo finally admitted that he had never been more than a *donado*. At some point worldly "appetites," as he would call them, overtook Atondo's spiritual fervor: he was carried away by avarice and a now "obstinate heart."[5] He stopped praying and fasting, began to make himself stylish clothing, for which he appropriated convent funds without permission, and exchanged amorous letters with a woman, sending her little gifts of clothing, relics, and a rosary that did not belong to him.[6] He kept these guilty secrets from the Franciscans. Probably in 1808, he fell ill, made a mendacious confession, and, fearing he was about to be found out, fled the convent on a horse borrowed from a "generous gentleman" of the town, leaving word that he was going to Córdoba on an urgent errand. Instead, he returned to Mexico City and enlisted the assistance of relatives there without telling them what he had done.

The following two years were all too eventful. He soon proposed marriage to a young woman of modest means. Short of funds to pay for the church wedding, he persuaded his future in-laws to lend him their jewels, which he proceeded to pawn to cover the marriage fees and wedding finery. Shortly after the wedding he was arrested for this debt to his wife's parents, but was released, he said, when he made restitution. A daughter was born, but Atondo came to detest his wife and spent little time at home. He took up the tailor's trade again, but decided that manual labor was not for him. He stripped his wife of her possessions, including her best clothes, and abandoned her. Disowned by his relatives, homeless, and sick with running sores, he made do as a beggar. Quick to spend what he had, Atondo was destitute. Perhaps in 1811—again, he was vague about the year—he was arrested by the police for stealing a relative's silver spoon, a silk shawl, a fine pillow cover, and two tunics.[7] He assured the Inquisition that it was a trumped-up charge, but in order to win his freedom he agreed to rejoin the royal regiment of dragoons. He was released from jail and sent to Puebla for assignment. With insurgents in the War of Independence rising up in parts of rural central and western Mexico, this was not an easy situation, and Atondo apparently arrived in a panic.

At this point Atondo's account and chronology become sketchier and less credible, involving alleged persecution by insurgents. He wrote that the bishop of Puebla had granted him permission to return to the Franciscan college in Orizaba, but on the way to Orizaba he was captured by insurgents, suffered a cut on his left ear, and was taken on a long journey to José María Morelos's headquarters at Chilpancingo. (Morelos was not at Chilpancingo until 1813. Atondo's sequence of events seems to require an earlier date. It is hard to tell how much of his stories of persecution by the insurgents is embroidered or simply made up to appeal to his royalist audience.) There he was tried as a royalist and sentenced to presidio service in chains at Zacatula. Later, along with other prisoners, he was pardoned to commemorate a great victory achieved by Don Pedro (presumably he meant Mariano) Matamoros, but was forced to join the insurgents' San Lorenzo regiment commanded by Don Ramón Sesma for an attack on the city of Valladolid. On the way to Valladolid, Sesma ordered the recently pardoned troops held back to keep them from defecting once the battle began. During the confusion as the insurgents retreated from Valladolid, Atondo says he was freed by a Captain Juan Miñón.

It was now April 1815 by Atondo's reckoning. He made his way to the small Franciscan house at Tlalpujahua seeking to renew his association with the order. The guardian sent him on to the major missionary college headquarters at Querétaro (which had fifty-five friars in residence in 1826), where he was accepted again as one of the *donados*.[8] Except in the kitchen, he said he proved himself to be a reliable worker, pious and efficient. During his months in the Querétaro convent he was given responsible assignments, including escorting a group of choristers to Celaya, caring for another deranged friar, and, later that year, undertaking a risky alms-collecting mission back to the Tlalpujahua area. Atondo said that he volunteered for this assignment in order to prove his devotion to the college. But Franciscan witnesses later testified that he did not volunteer and was reluctant to go—not without reason, since insurgent bands still occupied parts of eastern Michoacán. Atondo wrote that when an insurgent detachment confronted him at San

José Buenavista, he told them he was a priest, hoping this would protect him from harm. It seemed to work, and he completed the ruse by tonsuring himself—shaving the crown of his head—and starting to confess penitents, celebrate Mass, offer blessings, and grant indulgences as he continued the mission through the towns of San Felipe del Obraje, Tapaxco, and Taximaroa. But insurgents in the area soon seized his possessions and sent him to their leader, Ignacio Rayón, at Pátzcuaro. He said he was held in a cave and then moved with Rayón's troops to El Cóporo, a remote encampment east of Dolores Hidalgo, Guanajuato, where he was imprisoned and tried as a royalist spy.

In his written confession to the Inquisition, Atondo went on at length in heroic terms about his captivity, describing a stirring encounter with his prosecutor and judge, a rebel Franciscan-now-colonel whom he likewise fooled into believing that he, too, was a Franciscan priest. The prosecutor demanded to know whether he was a lay brother or a priest, to which he replied that he was a priest on an innocent mission to collect alms for his needy fellow Franciscans in Querétaro. Then the prosecutor asked Atondo why he didn't serve the insurgent American Nation—"which, in my mind, God would regard as a betrayal of the Fatherland"—and stop collecting alms for royalists.[9] To that, Atondo said, he replied that under no circumstances would he join them because that would make him an apostate, deserving excommunication: "[I told them] that I pray the commandments of the Laws of God as they were meant, not the opposite, as would be done there."[10] Rayón broke in at this point, wanting to know why Atondo dared to respond to his (Rayón's) colonel "with such impudence and disrespect, to which I replied that for me he was not a colonel, but my brother, a fellow son of my father St. Francis."[11] According to Atondo, after this daring response, Rayón and his Franciscan-colonel decided to release him, on the condition that he promise not to divulge anything about the El Cóporo encampment: "Seeing that he could not persuade me . . . he realized that I would be . . . a harmful influence and would seduce the soldiers into deserting that unjust cause."[12]

Atondo found his way to Tuxpan, in the eastern corner of Michoacán, near the pine-oak forests that are home to a famous monarch butterfly refuge, and then east to San Felipe del Obraje, today's San Felipe del Progreso. The pastor of San Felipe reported that Atondo lodged with him during his visit to collect alms, and again referred to himself as a priest. Several days later, the pastor said he learned that Atondo had spent the alms he collected there on gambling and binge drinking in a public tavern. He heard from a servant accompanying Atondo that in Tuxpan Atondo had sought permission from the parish priest to celebrate Mass but had been denied because the license he presented was only for collecting alms, but that on the road from Tuxpan, at a place called Los Trojes, Atondo had confessed a gravely ill woman. Atondo would later firmly deny to the Inquisition that he had drunk to excess in a public tavern or gambled away the alms he had collected, but admitted that he had confessed a woman during his travels as an act of charity.

According to the parish priest of Chapa de Mota, a town southeast of Querétaro, another three days' travel east of San Felipe, Atondo appeared there on July 9 requesting lodging and permission to collect alms. He introduced himself as a distant relative of the priest and said that he had come from El Cóporo, where insurgents had held him captive. The priest said he had never heard of Atondo before. As he listened to Atondo's outpouring of incoherent words, he wondered whether he might be a spy. That night Atondo grew more expansive, telling everyone in the household that he was an ordained Franciscan friar, first a Fernandino in Mexico City, then a Dieguino at Orizaba, where he had been seized by insurgents under "someone named" ("un tal") Arroyo when rebels loyal to Morelos passed through; that he had been sent to Zacatula as a prisoner, then freed in a general pardon granted by Morelos when his congress was convened at Chilpancingo; and other lies. When asked for his licenses to celebrate Mass and confess, Atondo replied that the insurgents had destroyed them, so the priest told him that he could not perform the duties of a priest there. When he was about to head north the three leagues or so to Xilotepec, the priest of Chapa de Mota confronted him with the fact that his license to collect alms had the word "layco" (layperson) scratched out where the licensee was identified. Atondo replied that originally a *layco* was supposed to undertake the mission, but considering that the bandits would rob a layman, his prelate had appointed a priest to undertake the assignment. According to the priest of Chapa de Mota, Atondo continued to call himself a priest after he left town. He did not know whether Atondo had celebrated Mass or confessed anyone else.

On September 23 (still 1815), Atondo surfaced in the town of San Jerónimo Aculco, closer to San Juan del Río and Querétaro, now as a full-fledged priest impersonator with a string of Masses and confessions on his record. He wrote that he sought out the parish priest there to show him his licenses for alms collecting, but the priest waved them off and told him he could do as he pleased. When a subdeacon—a young man in minor orders—approached him in the parish church for confession, Atondo said he complied because he "saw the great need there for a priest from outside."[13] After confessing the subdeacon, Atondo said he celebrated Mass in the church and then went on confessing the many women and men who approached him. He said he urged them all to make a full and general confession, that they should not be ashamed before their priests, that it was God, not the priest, who would hear their confession and mete out divine justice on the Day of Judgment, that God was all-knowing and could not be deceived even in the most secret matters. He left Aculco (he did not say when) and headed for the Hacienda San Antonio because, he said, he realized he was committing a sin even though he was trying to heal those lost souls—none of whom had acquired the indulgences of a Bula de la Santa Cruzada, he emphasized—and lead them on the true path.[14]

Called to testify in October, soon after Atondo's arrest, the parish priest of Aculco told a different story. When Atondo presented himself on September 23 as a Franciscan from Querétaro collecting alms for his convent, the priest had welcomed him to the parish and offered him lodging. The next morning, a Sunday, when the priest went to church to celebrate Mass, he found Atondo confessing the subdeacon in the sacristy. They were still there when he finished the Mass. The priest went home and discovered a little later that Atondo had stayed behind to say Mass and confess some twenty-three people. That night he reprimanded Atondo for doing this without his permission and asked him for his licenses. Atondo replied that his licenses to celebrate Mass and confess had been destroyed by insurgents while he was held at El Cóporo, that he had only his license from his prelate in Querétaro to collect alms and his government pass to travel. In inspecting the license for alms collecting, the priest noticed that in the place where the collector's *estado religioso* (standing as a priest) was written, it read "de oficio layco" (layman's mission) and that someone had tried to scratch out the word "layco." Atondo's explanation again was that "layco" had been written by mistake and that his prelate had scratched it out.

The priest recognized that Atondo had been given a responsible assignment by his superior in the convent, but he knew then that Atondo was a layman, not a priest. He did not believe Atondo's story that he was really a missionary priest from the Colegio de Orizaba and wondered about his stories that two of his fellow Franciscans had been killed by insurgents while carrying out their mission, and that he himself was an ardent foe of the insurgency. Now suspicious, the priest told him to stop the Masses and confessions until he could prove he was licensed and immediately wrote to a fellow priest to whom Atondo claimed kinship, to determine whether Atondo was being truthful. This priest replied the next day, September 25, that he did not know Atondo and could not say whether he was a priest. The priest of Aculco immediately wrote to a Franciscan acquaintance in Querétaro, who replied on September 28 that Atondo had presented himself there as a friar from the Colegio Apostólico of Orizaba who had been imprisoned by insurgents at El Cóporo. The friars at Orizaba did not accept his claim to be ordained, but had employed Atondo in several jobs, and he had acquitted himself as an honorable man ("hombre de bien"), most recently in the alms collection mission. He added that Atondo's actions in Aculco were no doubt criminal and contrary to his position and it was untrue that the prelate would have scratched out the word *layco*. A second priest residing in Aculco testified that at first Atondo seemed a pious and politic man, praising the well-kept chapel and piety of the people, acting like an uncompromising patriot and speaking enthusiastically against the insurgents. But he also made doubtful boasts about having been a seminarian in Mexico City, being well known to the soldiers in three leading towns, and having confessed and absolved from excommunication a criminal who was about to be executed.

While his lies and impersonations were being exposed in Aculco, on Sunday morning, October 1, Atondo left town, reaching the hacienda settlement of San Antonio that afternoon. Meanwhile the priest of Aculco sent a message to the military commander at San Antonio that if Atondo traveled that way rather than to San Juan del Río he should be arrested and sent to Querétaro. The next day, Monday, October 2, Atondo was assuring people at San Antonio that he had ministered at Aculco with the consent of the parish priest and that the priest had verified his licenses and urged Atondo to confess several betrothed couples. Atondo proceeded to say Mass in the chapel at San Antonio, serve communion to sixteen adults in attendance, and, "against my will" ("contra toda mi voluntad") and feeling guilty, confess various people, including women who had followed him from Aculco. He asked the commander for an introduction to the hacienda owner, who he knew was a priest. The *hacendado*-priest gave him breakfast and then took him to a bedroom and asked to see his license to celebrate Mass, confess, and serve communion. Here Atondo's account becomes more muddled. Feeling confused and faint with fear, he told the priest to arrest him. The priest went to the commander and told him to detain Atondo, but the commander did not come for him that day. Not wishing to flee this time, despite the opportunity, Atondo rode his horse to the barracks, then rode out for breakfast and returned to the barracks in the evening. The next morning, October 4, he said goodbye to the commander and headed toward San Juan del Río, but when he stopped for breakfast two soldiers and a corporal rode up and arrested him on the commander's orders. They escorted him to the commander at San Juan del Río, who asked him if he was a priest. He admitted he was not. The next day, two Franciscans came in, he assumed to hear him confess his crime, which he did. But then, he explained, seeing all the people who had gathered there and shamed at the thought of their hearing of his crime and spreading the news among the lowest circles of society, he backtracked and claimed he was actually a priest named Fray Antonio Borja who had become an insurgent and thereby given up being a Christian, none of which was true. Nevertheless, determined to pay for his own enormous crimes, he voluntarily turned himself in to authorities of the Inquisition.

With Atondo's arrest, the formal case against him before the Inquisition began to play out. From mid-October 1815 to April 1816 reports and testimonies were solicited and received. None of the informants is named, but all are identified in other ways.[15] The reports came from nine priests who met Atondo in his travels or had information about him, including the two priests at Aculco, the parish priests of Chapa de Mota and San Felipe del Obraje, and five Franciscans from the convents in Querétaro and Orizaba and the Colegio de San Fernando in Mexico City. The sixteen witnesses were mainly citizens of Aculco who had attended the Masses Atondo celebrated and confessed to him (nine men and one woman, eight of them identified as *españoles*, one a local Indian noble, and one a *vecino* or resident of the town), but there were also three Franciscans, including a former guardian and a *donado* of the Colegio de San Fernando, and the distinguished senior preacher of the Colegio de Orizaba. The Inquisition chose not to seek witnesses from Atondo's earlier years.

In March 1816, Atondo made his preliminary confession in the imposing audience chamber of the Inquisition, a paneled, dimly lit hall with columns and drapery of silk damask and red velvet edged in gold, more than eighty feet long and twenty-two feet wide, before the Inquisitors seated in high-back chairs at their table on a raised platform.[16] Suitably impressed, he wrote out his long confession soon thereafter. In November 1816 there was another hearing in the Inquisitors' chambers, at which he was allowed to clarify his original oral confession. In October 1817 the long set of formal charges against Atondo was finally drawn up by the prosecuting Inquisitor. Atondo's responses to the formal charges are undated but must have been made before March 10, 1818, since the Inquisitors' hearing of Atondo's case on that date refers to them. Atondo's responses to the reports and witness testimonies also are undated, but would have been made after July 10, 1818, since the last dated record in the file refers to the hearing on that date in which Atondo responded to witness testimony. The last document in the file, Atondo's instructions to his defense attorney, is also undated but mentions that he had spent three years in the Inquisition's cells by that time, so it would postdate July 10, 1818. There is no record of completion of the trial, or sentence, or other notation. Perhaps Atondo died while still in custody. In any case, the paper trail ends there.

Atondo Presents Himself to the Inquisition

Until we lost sight of Juan Atondo in 1818 in the cells of the Inquisition at age thirty-five, his adult life was a wobbling succession of deceptions, betrayals, sudden departures, and nervy lies, punctuated by illness and regret. There is little sense of peace or satisfaction in his account of life as a sometime Dieguino novice; his failed apprenticeship in a tailor's shop in Mexico City; his two years as a soldier; at least two terms in jail for theft; three years serving in the Franciscan missionary college in Orizaba; brief marriage, parenthood, and another apprenticeship during two more years in Mexico City; then another shorter term as a soldier; two or three years in the company of insurgents; another year or more as a Franciscan servant, this time in Querétaro; another year, perhaps, of captivity by insurgents; some feverish months impersonating a priest; and, finally, his arrest near Aculco in 1815 and transfer to the custody of the Inquisition.

Mixed signals about Atondo's character and intentions during those years of erratic, sometimes criminal behavior complicate his presentation of his misadventures. Intense feelings pepper his accounts: desire, shame, sadness, remorse, despair, physical and mental anguish, zeal, heartache. The narrative of his life and the notes he made for his attorney are filled with words of raw emotion—his "flaming love [and] . . . desire" as a youth hoping to become a Dieguino; the anguish that washed over him for presuming to celebrate Mass; the shame he felt at his uncontrolled desires and appetites. "I say this with tears in my eyes and my pulse racing," he wrote at the end of his confession.[17] Judging by Atondo's accounts in 1816, he apparently was content and in good health only during his time in the Orizaba convent, even though he said he slept just two hours a night there, at most. Even at Orizaba, happy memories faded before his unruly appetites. And, of course, he left that convent abruptly, too.

To explain himself, Atondo repeatedly referred to his heart as an unruly force of its own that directed his behavior and usually betrayed him. The heart trope expressed his suffering and his deepest impulses, as it often did in texts on moral theology, although those texts were meant to point the way toward purity and serenity. Atondo wrote repeatedly of acting "with all my heart." On the verge of entering the convent at Orizaba, "my heart was afflicted." He wrote of his heart "weighing him down," of his "obstinate heart," of "my heart needing to be calmed," and of "the hidden motives of my heart," which he did not understand.[18] Atondo's written confession and responses to the charges and testimony entered against him expressed regret, contrition, and abject apology. These utterances while in the Holy Office's custody were directed as much to God as to the Inquisitors, and he certainly gave himself a rhetorical flogging: "my enormous crimes"; "[I am] a great sinner"; "my depraved malice and wickedness"; "my evil deeds" and "many dirty tricks," frauds, and swindles; "my evil life"; "such scandalous and criminal excesses"; "my stupid appetites." At an especially low point he cried out, "Up to now I have lived as a pagan . . . a devil"; "I became a devil"; "I am the worst in the world."[19] More than once he paused in his written confession and instructions to his attorney to "beg for pardon" or to assure the tribunal of his "genuine remorse."[20] He had suffered, as a great sinner must, he wrote, using the same stinging term, "congoja" (grief), to describe both Christ's anguish in the Passion and his own. He readily admitted to most of the many serious charges leveled against him—thirty-six in all. As sadness gave way to despair by the end of the prosecution's presentation to the tribunal and his years in prison, Atondo threw himself on the mercy of the court. "I implore your mercy," he wrote. "There is nothing more I can do but weep and repent my sins."[21]

Lies, many and various, were among the sins the penitent Atondo recalled in his long confession as proof of his earnest attempt now to tell the whole truth. In addition to posing as an ordained priest and assuming an alias, he admitted that he had lied to and stolen from relatives and his wife's parents, and that he had twice falsely claimed to be an apostate, hoping to be arrested by ecclesiastical authorities rather than constables for the king's high criminal court (Sala de Crimen). Other lies and boasts that Atondo skipped over came out in witness declarations: claiming that he had lost his written licenses to administer sacraments or that they had been confiscated and destroyed by insurgents; scratching out the word "layco" from his permit to collect alms for the Querétaro Franciscans and claiming that the document proved he was a priest; claiming he had been a student at the Franciscan seminary in Mexico City; telling acquaintances that he had confessed and absolved a condemned prisoner, then admitting it was just a boast when the Inquisition declared such an act to be an especially grievous violation of the sacrament. His biggest lie—which he refused to admit until authoritative witnesses declared otherwise—was that he had professed in the Franciscans' Orizaba convent and been accepted into minor orders.

Unruly urges were among his great regrets. Atondo wrote of his sometimes towering hunger for food—several times interrupting the confessional narrative to note that he stopped off for breakfast here or there, or was particularly hungry at some place. He also admitted to a weakness for stylish clothing that he made or stole—"a sordid avarice" ("sórdida avaricia") that was also evident in his distress at having his wardrobe confiscated when he was arrested, not to mention his coveting his wife's finery and abandoning her in her underclothes. He was less forthcoming about his carnal appetites, but did admit that they had drawn him into marriage after he left the Orizaba convent. When these urges came over him he "changed into a demon," and his customary "humility turned into arrogance."[22]

But among his appetites there keeps reappearing a thread of fervent, sometimes ecstatic religiosity that he called his "propensión religiosa" (religious inclination). His bleak, but oddly hopeful understanding of Christian theology and the presence of Satan served him to explain his temptations and sufferings. In the written confession, he presented his spiritual life as an almost epic drama, passing from light to darkness, with a ray of hope that he might be able to return to the light. He presented his sufferings in almost biblical terms, as God's punishment for his sins—himself mocked, as Christ was mocked; his running sores almost Job-like; his anguish akin to Christ's Passion.[23]

The Devil loomed, and here the Inquisition agreed, seeing an "espíritu infernal" (infernal spirit) in his seduction of penitents.[24] One night while he was in Puebla in 1813, after abandoning his wife and being struck down with leprous-like sores, he cried out to the Devil with all his heart, as he had heard others say they did: "Come, my friend, and I will give you what you work so hard to achieve in taking a soul." At that point he thought about taking off his string of rosary beads and crushing them underfoot, "but the Sovereign Queen and Mother of Sinners would not let me do it. Instead I kissed it and felt fear." Pulled back from the brink by this epiphany, he said he came to see his suffering as God's punishment: "that God, as a good father, tried to inspire me, and I had refused to obey."[25] His *propensión religiosa* coming to the fore, he soon made a confession and sought the bishop's permission to return to the Orizaba convent. But this would not turn out to be his road to Damascus, after all; on the road thither, insurgents captured him.

The act of confession is a key to Atondo's fraught relationship with his *propensión religiosa*—his urge to confess others and his resistance to making a full confession himself. In passing, he admitted more than once to hiding his crimes, to having made incomplete and otherwise deceitful confessions, as he did in preparation for his marriage, or to avoiding confession altogether when he knew he had serious sins to account for. When arrested in 1815, he conceded that he had not confessed in two years, but he assured the Inquisition that he had made a good confession of his entire life in 1813 after hearing a sermon about God's mercy that "filled me with courage and confidence that all my sins would be forgiven."[26] (The Inquisition's prosecutor was not persuaded, noting that this confession would have been tailored to his need for the bishop's permission for him to return to the Orizaba convent, which would not have been granted if all of Atondo's many sins had been told.) Atondo said more than once that the long account of his life and sins written in the Inquisition cells was a candid and full confession. Writing at such length, identifying many scandalous sins, he may have thought of it as a thorough accounting, but it contains obvious obfuscations and omissions. In it Atondo continued to swear that he had professed and had been accepted into the novitiate at Orizaba, even though he had already admitted orally to his captor near Aculco, and would later admit to the Inquisition as well, that this was a lie. Again, he denied scratching out the word "layco," which identified him as a layman, on his permit to collect alms for the Querétaro Franciscans. He insisted that people had flocked to him for confession, that he had actively encouraged no one. One lay witness from Aculco disputed this claim, but the others who praised him show that he profited from a reservoir of unmet demand for confession.[27] His two extended stretches of time among insurgents led to the suspicion that he was an insurgent sympathizer, if not a member. Was he the fervent royalist he repeatedly claimed to be? Did he really argue with Ignacio Rayón and live to tell the tale? We have only Atondo's word for it.

Atondo had a problem of his own with truth telling in the confessional, but he was eager to act as confessor to dozens of other laypeople during his impersonation of a priest in 1815. He had prepared himself for the opportunity by devouring a standard guide for confessors, Cristóbal de Vega's *Casos raros de la confesión, con reglas y modo fácil para hacer una buena confesión general o particular* . . . (Notable cases from the confessional, with rules and easy ways to make a good general or particular confession . . .).[28] And to all appearances, he did a conscientious job, both in reassuring penitents and warning them with hair-raising stories from Vega of divine retribution for imperfect confessions. The five male witnesses from Aculco who said he had confessed them took him to be an experienced and competent spiritual judge, a "confesor bueno." One said he was a good confessor "because he scrutinized my conscience according to the Commandments of God and the Church, and because of his exhortations that were meant to arouse true feelings of charity."[29] Gliding over his own lost soul, Atondo even seemed to persuade himself that he was not a fraud. Rather, he regarded these confessions as righteous acts of charity: "Thanks to my advice, those souls that had lost the true path were healed."[30]

Atondo described in detail his long, probing confession of the young subdeacon of Aculco: "And so, deciding to confess him, I sat down in the sacristy and he knelt before me."[31] Atondo told him that as a future confessor himself, he should not be too troubled since priests were sinners too, and that he should calm his heart and unburden himself fully and sincerely, placing himself in God's hands for forgiveness. He told the subdeacon to probe his conscience for any sins he had not revealed before, and that if he needed convincing he should read *Casos raros de la confesión*, where he would find many examples of the results of a bad confession. For the young man's edification, Atondo extracted one of the volume's chilling stories:

A seminarian denounced himself in the confessional for sins of dishonesty, but, in doing so, he failed to confess one of these sins. He did many penances, his teacher loved him very much for his virtues, and his fellow students esteemed him. When he fell deathly ill, he was given the sacraments and, with tears in his eyes—which they took to be tears of contrition—he died denouncing himself. His teacher wanted to know what fate befell him, so he prayed for him. His student appeared, sighing deeply and saying, "Do not pray for me, I am damned." The teacher asked how that could be, considering all his penances? The student replied that he had, indeed, done so, but that, out of shame, he withheld one sin in his confession, "for which I damned myself, as you can see."[32]

After telling this story, Atondo implored the young man to remember Christ's Passion and that Christ sweated blood in his sorrow and anguished prayers before he was crucified, not because of the pain He would suffer, but for the evil that men were about to do Him. "[I told him] many other things and he began his confession. Seeing his suffering and contrition, and recognizing myself as a sinner, too, I was confounded and realized [what was happening]. . . . [After he finished, I ended by] telling him more about Christ's Passion and the Sorrows of Most Holy Mary. He wept copiously, shedding many tears, which persuaded me that what I had done . . . out of brotherly desire was good."[33]

Why did Atondo have this urge to confess others in 1815? Was he carried away by his *propensión religiosa*, his sometime compassion for others in emotional and spiritual distress, and a growing sense of mission? His explanation to the Inquisition was that he was inspired by the time he spent as Rayón's prisoner, where "I saw the Catholic Faith completely lost, that this moved me to do what I did."[34] But perhaps he was also driven by curiosity about the secret lives and sins of others, or had wanted reassurance that others also experienced uncontrollable desires? Perhaps he was trying to summon the courage to finally make a full confession of his own before a sympathetic confessor? At one point in his written confession he wondered what was really in his heart in wanting to confess others. Was it charity, or pride and the gratification of posing as a benign figure of authority in his Franciscan habit?

As contrite as he seemed to be when he wrote his confession, and as many times as he rebuked himself for his great sins, lamented ignoring God's messages to him, and declared that he deserved the harshest punishment,[35] Atondo held out hope that he would be forgiven or at least treated with mercy and moderation. To that end he included as many mitigating circumstances and justifications for his actions as he could think of. Here and there he appealed to the Inquisitors to consider his merits, especially his religious ardor and loyalty to the crown, and his suffering from illness, want, mockery, and peril at the hands of insurgents. He assured the tribunal that he had now made a full confession and promised to change his ways and spend the rest of his life in devoted service to God. Glossing over his desertion, Atondo noted that he had been obedient and diligent in his time in the military, in the Orizaba and Querétaro convents, and in prison; he had not resisted arrest or tried to escape; he had had the best of charitable intentions in confessing penitents and had committed this sacrilege reluctantly, bending to their fervent and anxious entreaties. Celebrating Mass was harder to justify, but he insisted that he had done it only twice. Among Rayón's men, he suggested, his imposture even risked a kind of martyrdom: "If it all improved because of my example, I did so gladly, resigned to suffer whatever may please God and Your Highness." At this point in his confession, Atondo evidently sensed that he had gone overboard; he added that while "it seemed to him that he acted out of charity, it could also have been out of arrogance and self-regard."[36]

Atondo became more confused as his reasons multiplied. But his most insistent explanation was that he had acted out of ignorance, unaware that his offenses were so serious: "When I committed my crimes I did not know they would come before the Inquisition, although I was not unaware that they were bad because, knowing they were sins, I should not have committed them."[37] No matter how grave his sins might be, Atondo seemed to think he would be forgiven and maybe the Inquisition would release him from prison. He said that a homily delivered by a Jesuit priest in Puebla had filled him with the expectation that he would be forgiven in the here and now, and renewed his desire to serve Christ by returning to the Orizaba convent. The Jesuit spoke of Christ's mercy and all that He had suffered in order to free the faithful from eternal damnation:

A few days later we traveled on to Puebla. . . . Upon arrival, I set about reconsidering and looking within myself. One night, more out of curiosity than devotion, I went to the spiritual exercises that the Jesuits conduct in their church. There I heard a homily that seemed directed especially to me, emphasizing God's Mercy and His great suffering in order to free us from eternal damnation, and however many our sins, His Mercy is far greater, and that a single drop of the blood He shed for us on the Cross was enough to save us. . . . With this, I became filled with strength and confidence that all my sins would be forgiven.[38]

The Inquisitors and Others Appraise Juan Atondo

There is less to say about the Inquisitors' estimation of Atondo and his deeds and motives since the dossier lacks a final judgment and sentence, and the tribunal failed to investigate whether he had indeed been a royalist in insurgent hands. But there is enough to conclude that the judges had a categorical view of the case and were little interested in the ambiguities, asides, and doubtful claims floating through Atondo's account of himself. The prosecuting Inquisitor understandably doubted the complete truthfulness of his written confession. The lies, other sins, and tall tales were too glaring and too serious to get a sympathetic hearing, especially impersonating a priest at the altar and in the confessional. For the prosecuting Inquisitor, it was a question of good and evil, and he did not find much goodness in Atondo's words and actions. By his reckoning, Atondo was a heretic ("hereje formal") and an apostate from Our Catholic Religion ("apóstata de Nuestra Religión Católica"). The litany of accusations went on: Atondo was a devil worshiper ("pactario"), a rebel of his own free will ("rebelde voluntario"), a perjurer, a deluded liar, an ignorant evildoer ("ignorante malvado"), a libertine, a source of public scandal ("público escandaloso") and sacrileges, a man of vice-ridden habits, and possibly a closet insurgent.

In the prosecuting Inquisitor's opinion, Atondo showed no respect for the religion into which he had been baptized and educated, and which he claimed to profess. Whatever spark of Christian piety there might have been had been extinguished by what Atondo called his "appetites" and the Inquisitor considered his deadly sins—his lust ("luxuria") and sordid avarice ("sórdida avaricia").

Atondo had ignored God's warnings to him—the illnesses and skin eruptions he suffered, and the times he was incarcerated and stripped of his meager possessions—and had flouted God's goodness. Atondo did not try to refute this judgment.

Like Atondo, the prosecutor used the heart as a metaphor to describe and explain the accused's behavior, but he did so in a more damning, doctrinal way. Atondo had recognized in passing that the heart is the site of divine love, but he spoke of his heart mainly as inflamed by unruly, uncontrollable emotions. He said more than once that he did not know his own heart. Only once, in his youth, had he "understood and acted upon his heart's true desire," when he decided to join the Dieguinos.[39] To the prosecutor, the heart was the living organ of God's boundless love, burning with goodness, compassion, and contrition. It was the seat of the faithful's conscience and moral strength—heartache purifies. To the prosecutor, Atondo's "violent, heretical impulses evidenced an extremely weak and corrupt heart."[40]

Many of the Inquisition's charges against Atondo concerned the confessions he heard. In spite of the chorus of satisfied confessees from Aculco, the prosecuting Inquisitor took a dim view of Atondo's assertion that he had performed a charitable service by confessing them and others:

> Even though those who were confessed by this offender assure us that he seemed to be a good confessor because of the advice and examples he gave . . . we deduce that he behaved with excessive indiscretion and imprudence that would cause grave harm to this same sacrament. . . . And he broadcast that he had confessed someone who was going to be executed, absolving him of excommunication.[41]

This sacrilege compromised the well-being of souls and their salvation: "[His] excessive indiscretion and negligence . . . would cause grave harm to this very sacrament of health." Atondo's activity as a confessor was the ultimate expression of his "lack of respect for the religion he professes."[42] Even if Atondo actually considered himself a priest—and the Inquisitor seemed to believe that he was genuinely deluded in this way—his supposed remark that a layperson could administer the sacrament of penance in special circumstances heretically echoed Luther in elevating the laity to the same level of authority and power ("potestad") as ordained priests, and was a proposition condemned by the Council of Trent, the Inquisitor noted.

Equally galling to the tribunal was Atondo's insistence that he had professed in minor orders with the Franciscans of Orizaba:

Even in the cells of the Inquisition he has continued to call himself a *religioso* [member of a religious order], has had himself tonsured and signs his declarations with the title of Fray Juan Atondo, inflicting great harm on this Tribunal and depreciating its authority, as if it was not capable of discovering . . . his deceptions and determining exactly that Atondo has not been other than a lowly servant who did not profess.[43]

Another grave error was Atondo's complacent view of God's mercy and forgiveness:

He convinced himself that what he did was good, that contrite penitents believing that he was a priest thought they would be pardoned by the word of Jesus Christ, that if they were contrite they would instantly be forgiven and placed in the grace of God no matter if they had committed the gravest sins in the world.[44]

In the prosecutor's opinion, Atondo was a lost sheep, not the prodigal son he claimed to be. He was a hypocrite and opportunist governed by sin. His "profession" as a priest was either a "diabolical illusion" or the product of "consummate hypocrisy, meant to deceive."[45] But given that the tribunal proceeded to hold him in the Inquisition cells for about three years, rather than moving promptly to a verdict and sentence after gathering evidence and taking depositions, it would appear that something more than Atondo's personal transgressions was involved. In that time of political upheaval in both Spain and Mexico, his erratic behavior and misguided religious zeal were greater, potentially more threatening to the faith and the crown than Aguayo's cynical impersonations and schemes to escape. It must have seemed best to keep him out of circulation.

In their reports and testimony, other priests who witnessed Atondo's spree of Masses and confessions, or knew him in Querétaro, or knew of him in Orizaba and Mexico City had nothing positive to add on his behalf. Nor, with one exception, did they make observations that might help us imagine him as much more than a demon or a garrulous liar. In hindsight, they regarded him as a sly, evasive character and did not believe his claim to have professed in Orizaba. The exception was the pastor of Chapa de Mota, who considered Atondo a strangely troubled person, confused in his thinking and unreliable.

Conclusion: His Propensión Religiosa

Juan Atondo is not an open book. For all that he wrote and said for the record about himself and his feelings, much remains unresolved about his activities and motives. To who, or to what, was he loyal? More than a few people did him a good turn, but there are no signs of reciprocal, lasting gratitude. Was it poverty that drove him to petty crime and all the betrayals and departures? His aversion to work, inclination to spend beyond his means, and sudden departures from the Dieguino novitiate, military service, and the Franciscan convent at Orizaba when he was not strapped for money or in debt suggest that poverty alone does not explain his conduct. What were his physical ailments? Do they account in any way for his behavior? Was he the dissolute drunkard and gambler one of the parish priests he met in 1815 took him to be? Was he the ardent royalist he claimed to be, or an ambivalent insurgent, or neither? Did he rebuke an insurgent chief, as he claimed? If he *was* released from the insurgent camp at El Cóporo, why? From circumstantial evidence the Inquisitors suspected he was an insurgent sympathizer, but they chose not to investigate.

Even if Atondo's written and spoken words for the Inquisition were not simply spontaneous, the raw emotions that rise from the pages of his dossier were a way to show the Inquisitors that his contrition was real and heartfelt, that he *was* the prodigal son come home. His meandering written confession reads like a kind of psychotherapy, talking through his erratic behavior as a means of control over his mysterious impulses and reassurance of his sanity and moral responsibility. The urgency in his words, the confusion, contradictions, outrageous boasts and lies, and vivid memories of desire and suffering since his boyhood suggest that what he reveals there of his state of mind was more than a courtroom ploy. Although he sometimes seemed to be a phony and a hypocrite in obvious ways,[46] his words are more than a screen carefully set up to hide his true feelings. As he said, he did not know his own unruly heart, and seemed genuinely confused by some of what he had done. Perhaps he meant to clear his conscience of his many sins, but clung to a central lie about his own identity, that he had been received as a Franciscan novice at Orizaba.

Atondo presented himself as torn between "apetitos torpes" (stupid, greedy appetites) and a *propensión religiosa*. Whatever it amounted to, this self-proclaimed *propensión religiosa* was the one lasting thread of hope in his life story, from his desire as a teenager to become a Dieguino to his service in the Orizaba convent and imagined profession, his epiphany about forgiveness in Puebla, his attempted return to the convent in Orizaba, his study of the pastoral text on confession, his later service at the Querétaro college convent, and his final alms-collecting mission that turned into a spree of confessions, blessings, and Masses. Whether and when his *propensión religiosa* drove his actions, and whether or when he actually regarded himself as a priest, is beyond what we can conclude with much confidence. But there is clearly more to Atondo's understanding of his bursts of religious fervor than the Inquisition's categories of evil, heresy, or sincere Christianity, and more than an ephemeral conviction that even if he was not formally ordained, he was the equal of priests in the sight of God, having been fortified by the Virgin Mary. It is something Atondo does not try to explain beyond asserting that this conviction was "not because of the power I had, which was none, but by the word of Jesus Christ which schools us in fraternal hope that through contrition he may have it [forgiveness] even if he has committed the gravest sins."[47] Perhaps Atondo's understanding is best conveyed in Rudolf Otto's view that the source of religion is not only in the moral imperatives expressed in commandments and doctrinal teachings, but in an ineffable but visceral experience of exaltation from a sense that one is accompanied by a divine presence.[48]

Whatever part Atondo's *propensión religiosa* played in his baffling behavior over nearly twenty years, the observations of the pastor of

Chapa de Mota shortly after meeting Atondo the putative priest on his alms-collecting mission in 1815 may come closest to taking his measure. On November 15 of that year, this pastor reported that Atondo was "a man of two tongues, who only tries to flatter and seem to agree with everyone." His nervous manner and "torrent of words and the disconnected, often contradictory threads of his conversation" had immediately struck him as strange.[49] Here, thought the pastor, was a "persona de mala fe" (a person of bad faith)—an ambiguous phrase that could mean a person of suspect beliefs, but also a person who could not be trusted by others or himself.

Given the opportunity to reply to this pastor's appraisal of his character and mental state, Atondo was surprisingly mute, but in the appeal for clemency that he wrote out for his attorney, he wondered about the "illness I suffer from" ("la enfermedad que padezco") which, like his *propensión religiosa*, was more than he could untangle and put into words. Chapter 4 has more to say about this illness.

3 Protean Pícaros

My first reading of Joseph Aguayo's Inquisition files brought to mind José Joaquín Fernández de Lizardi's fictional Periquillo Sarniento, Mexico's "mangy parrot," a twist on his Christian name, Pedro Sarmiento, and an apt nickname for this restless young idler and cheat.[1] Fernández de Lizardi's Periquillo is one in a line of Hispanic literary *pícaros* reaching back to Lazarillo de Tormes, Guzmán de Alfarache, and Francisco de Quevedo's Don Pablos (*el buscón*, "the grifter") in the sixteenth and seventeenth centuries. All these characters are small-time impostors, swindlers, and thieves, social outcasts lied to and living on lies and the credulity of others. They are errant rogues, but rarely vicious, performers and persuaders meant to stir in readers a certain apprehension and revulsion mixed with wonder, and an occasional belly laugh, or at least a smile of recognition and perhaps hope for their redemption. Some style themselves the poor man's *hidalgo*—disdainful of manual labor, beholden to no one, and touchy about their honor—but they are warped and unsettling parodies of the model *hidalgo*, that Christian knight-errant of honor in search of adventure, righting wrongs, and defending the helpless. Are similarities between the two eighteenth-century priest impersonators and these young rogues of Early Modern fiction instructive? Is art imitating life here, or the other way around? Or are the resemblances just coincidental? Did Joseph Aguayo and Juan Atondo think of themselves—or did the authorities and a wider public think of them—in ways shaped by picaresque models? These questions loom large, but the answers are elusive. They are easier asked than answered because reception of popular ideas and texts is seldom well documented in the Early Modern written record, and just what "pícaro" meant to people then is no simple matter.

Early Literary Pícaros

"A vagabond is a newcomer in a heap of trouble"

—JAMES TATE[2]

Looking for answers in the early novels and secondary literature proved instructive, but less conclusive than I had hoped. Early picaresque fiction is a wide-open category for most literary historians and a nearly closed one for others, in good part because the varied forms and characters regarded as picaresque escape a narrow definition. It is not surprising that the entry for the word *pícaro* in eighteenth-century editions of the Real Academia de la Lengua's dictionary includes several different meanings: deceitful, sly, skillful at deception, shameless and without honor, indecent, cruel, and heartless, but also cheerful, pleasant, witty, and fluent—at once or separately dishonest, dangerous, and endearing. A favorite trope among literary scholars of early picaresque novels and their protagonists is Proteus, the elusive old man of the sea in Greek mythology who surrenders his wisdom grudgingly. He constantly changes form, from tree to water to serpent, in order to hide from his pursuers, who must "grasp him steadfastly and press him yet the more" before he will assume his proper form and part with what he knows. "And," warns Joseph Campbell, "he never discloses everything. He will reply only to the question put to him."[3] In a protean spirit, Howard Mancing asked what a picaresque novel is, and answered with more questions. Is it a comic biography? A fictional autobiography? A realistic novel? A satiric novel?[4] And, I might add, is it little more than entertainment, with a cast of fools under observation for humorous purposes? Or is it also a weighty moral tale? Could it be all or most of these things at the same time?

Literary scholars are also not of one mind about whether the novels are mainly about poverty or not; whether they mainly express elite fear and abhorrence of marginalized, destitute, idle strangers or render audible the voice of the poor against the rich; whether they are Counter-Reformation tracts, entertainments with little religious content, or Erasmian humanist satires against moral and religious hypocrisy; whether the protagonist is a buffoon or a rebel who rejects society and its rewards, an anarchist or a social climber, an optimist or a pessimist; whether he (or sometimes she) is a hero to a large or small circle of readers, an antihero, or a nonhero.[5] The answers depend on suppositions about an author's intent and the audience, both the readers and the consumers of stories from the novels.

While as many as thirty Spanish works written in the sixteenth, seventeenth, and eighteenth centuries have been proposed as picaresque novels, only four early ones are widely accepted—*La vida de Lazarillo de Tormes y de sus fortunas y adversidades; La vida del pícaro Guzmán de Alfarache; La vida del buscón, llamado Don Pablos;* and *La vida y hechos de Estebanillo González, hombre de buen humor, compuesta por él mismo.* And for several leading scholars, these four are singular works rather than the backbone of a genre, their differences more important than their similarities.[6] The most often cited reflection on the problem of defining *lo picaresco* is an essay by Claudio Guillén, but Guillén does not, in fact, offer a definition. His target, as he puts it, is "a series of literary works, not a definition." He aims "to delineate as clearly as possible an object of study . . . [that is] flexible enough to allow for alterations in the works over time and different countries."[7] He writes of a picaresque genre as an ideal type that blends several early works and is warranted mainly because Miguel de Cervantes and a few other writers in the seventeenth century recognized it as a kind of literature.

As Guillén suggests, these early picaresque novels read like studies in human degradation. They are first-person "lives" in a soiled, pungent, shifting world, told in a series of episodes by a footloose young rogue who is usually short of money and friends. He quickly loses his innocence, learning to survive ruthlessly by his wits, distrust authority (especially law enforcement), and avoid honest labor whenever possible. He is a quick study and a font of impertinent jokes, pranks, and schemes to fool, confuse, and take what he wants from the trusting. He is absorbed in his immediate needs and appetites—the next meal, money, fine clothes, shelter, gambling, sex. He works to stay a step ahead of his victims and enemies, but is himself assaulted, robbed, and betrayed. He travels to new places and rubs elbows with different kinds of people, most of them from the shady lower reaches of the social order. He has a succession of masters, but comes to trust no one completely. Living in a self-conscious age of deception when it was best to remain flexible and wary, he would have warmed to the Jesuit author Baltasar Gracián's advice to "neither esteem nor abhor forever. Confide in your friends today as if they were your worst enemies tomorrow. . . .

And with your enemies always leave open the door to reconciliation."⁸ But in most of the celebrated early picaresque novels there is at least the possibility of reform and a sunlit redemption as the story unfolds. Few picaresque novels are presented as religious tracts, but the moral lessons in them and the *pícaro*'s redemption announce their Counter-Reformation roots. The guiding themes are transience, deception, freedom, survival, and change that *might* become transformation; but freedom and change are contingent and incomplete. The *pícaro* is a work in progress, more easily recognized by his impersonations and deceptions and the people he interacts with than by who he is and where he is headed, making the picaresque genre a vehicle suited to moral commentary as well as satirical entertainment.

Why did this kind of literature develop in Spain in the mid-sixteenth century and enjoy its creative peak and greatest popularity there in the early seventeenth century, with later echoes in the Americas? One answer views literary *pícaros* as immersed in the prevailing poverty, vagabondage, idleness, and duplicity of the lower classes of the time in Spain, playing on the anxieties of Old Christian readers, whether hereditary elite or nouveau riche, who were anxious about social turmoil and economic crisis.⁹ Vagabonds were automatically suspected of being criminals, or at best dishonest, thieving *pícaros*. In this view, the decline of the genre represented by shallow, cowardly Estebanillo González in the mid-seventeenth century reflected the tastes of an emerging bourgeois audience that wanted entertainment and progress, without the sermons on sin, original or otherwise. The three most celebrated novels—*La vida de Lazarillo de Tormes y de sus fortunas y adversidades*, *La vida del pícaro Guzmán de Alfarache*, and *La vida del buscón, llamado Don Pablos*—appeared before the end of Castile's time of prosperity and expansion in the late sixteenth and early seventeenth centuries, not during the steep downward spiral that was plain to all by the 1640s, when Spain's ongoing wars merged with the Thirty Years' War and caused devastation and violent political struggles on the Iberian Peninsula. But the prosperity of the sixteenth century did not prevent widespread social and political disorder that threatened established rules and privileges and added to a heightened sense of moral corruption and apocalyptic expectations. The bonanza of silver and gold from American mines was a mixed blessing, contributing to inflation and altering traditional ideas about usury and the circle of mutual dependence of rich and poor expressed in alms giving and other acts of charity. Many of the transient Iberians were lumped with gypsies, Jews, and Turks as disreputable characters out of place, while crimes against persons and property were a growing problem. Many newly incorporated subjects of the crown became strangers in a different sense. Were the *moriscos* (converted Muslims), *marranos* (converted Jews), and new Christians in the colonies who they appeared to be, or were they weak-willed pretenders and subversives? The early literary *pícaros* embodied a provocative social type emerging from a world turned upside down as life and privilege became increasingly precarious for Spaniards during the seventeenth century. Much as Baltasar Gracián saw it, Spain was living in an age of *engaño*—of illusion and disillusion—in which things were rarely what they seemed and relationships were fluid and open to betrayal and calamity. No one could be trusted absolutely.

Lazarillo de Tormes

La vida de Lazarillo de Tormes y de sus fortunas y adversidades, first published in the early 1550s and of unknown authorship, was something new for its time in European literature. Instead of an epic romance of chivalry and adventure, allegory of courtly love, or hagiography of a saint or monarch, here was an abbreviated life of a poor boy on the way to becoming a shameless man, setting out on a string of droll episodes of misfortune, hardship, and betrayal that both describe Lazarillo's trajectory as an antihero akin to Atondo and cast satirical light on the lower reaches of society and immorality through the characters he meets and serves in this world of want and abundance. Above all, Lazarillo is a perpetually hungry servant who finds himself supporting his various masters rather than being supported by them, as good masters should.

The novel tracks him through nine masters, most of them parsimonious and greedy, with one brief period of independent employment as a town crier. Lazarillo's mother becomes a homeless widow when he is eight years old. A few years later she gives him over to a blind beggar, advising him to "try to be good, and may God be your guide"—but within days, the sly beggar plays a trick on him and cracks his skull: "At that very instant . . . I awoke from the simplicity I had been sleeping in like a child. . . . I'm on my own now."[10] Raising his sights slightly, he goes on to serve a cruel priest who has no use for the golden rule; an inept and destitute squire; a Mercedarian friar; an unscrupulous seller of phony papal indulgences; a master tambourine painter; a chaplain whom he serves for four years as a water carrier, making just enough money to buy himself a gentleman's outfit and move on; and a constable. Finally he comes into better luck, at a price. He serves the archpriest of San Salvador, who arranges for him to marry the archpriest's servant and lover. Unmoved by the gossip that he is being cuckolded, at the end of the book Lazarillo has settled into the comforts of regular meals, a bed, and a roof over his head: "In those days I was in my prosperity and at the summit of all good fortune."[11]

Despite being reprinted several times in the 1550s, with many editions and steady popularity from 1599 to the nineteenth century, when it became the most widely known picaresque novel, *Lazarillo de Tormes* did not immediately inspire a literary genre. Although the book was not anti-religion or anti-Catholic, in 1559 it was banned by the Inquisition. Reprintings of the original text continued to appear in the seventeenth and eighteenth centuries, but an expurgated version that first appeared in Spain in 1573 would become the most available and frequently reprinted version in Spain before 1800.[12] Not until after 1599 was *Lazarillo de Tormes* followed by other picaresque novels.

Guzmán de Alfarache

La vida de Lazarillo de Tormes came into its own enduring popularity after 1599 thanks to the publication that year of the first part of *La vida del pícaro Guzmán de Alfarache* by Mateo Alemán. Most scholars agree that throughout the seventeenth and eighteenth centuries these quite different novels together were the touchstone for other literary works in a picaresque genre in Spain, and also in Germany, France, and England.[13] *Guzmán de Alfarache* was a much longer and more ambitious, intricate book, a moral treatise as much as a panoramic, satirical, first-person tale of a young rogue's life. It was also, as Guillén puts it, "one of the first authentic best sellers in the history of printing," with at least eighteen editions published between 1599 and 1683, thousands of copies shipped to the New World, and translations into German, French, and English.[14] Irving Leonard concluded that throughout the seventeenth and eighteenth centuries in

Spanish America, *Guzmán de Alfarache* and *Don Quixote* "retained a reading public probably exceeding that of any other work of prose fiction."[15]

Guzmán de Alfarache established the general plotline of travel, encounters, and episodes in a young man's prolonged delinquency after his father's death, in which: (1) An innocent youth strikes out on his own without a moral compass, pushed out on the road by poverty but also restless and ambitious to make his way in the world, to stand out. (2) Within days he is robbed, lied to, and betrayed. Out of shame, he refuses to return home. With mounting cynicism and no settled loyalties except to himself and his appetites, he sinks into a life of petty crime, occasional menial labor, posturing, and deception at the expense of others. There are ups and downs, but he survives at the margins of society, becoming predator more than prey. (3) At the end of the novel Guzmán undergoes a moral transformation and reunion with society framed in Christian terms. Much of the novel is taken up with incidents in his feverish quest for wealth, status, and revenge that take the reader along the seamy margins of towns and cities across Spain and Italy. We find him in Madrid, Toledo, Genoa, Rome, Florence, Milan, Genoa again, Barcelona, Madrid again, Alcalá, and Cádiz, and then in penal servitude on a galley at sea. For a time he is a university student, assistant cook, porter, personal servant to an army captain, beggar, attendant to a French ambassador and then a cardinal, the "friend" of a kindly Mercedarian friar, and administrator of a wealthy lady's estate, as well as a serial thief and swindler. He marries twice, prostituting his second wife, who then runs off with a ship's captain. He is finally arrested and sentenced to six years in the galleys for defrauding his wealthy employer. On shipboard he is falsely accused of theft by a fellow prisoner and nearly executed, but he proves his "goodness, innocence, and loyalty" to the captain, and that he is a changed man. His evil ways are over: "I would rather be torn to a hundred pieces than commit even the smallest worldly crime."[16]

The end of Guzmán de Alfarache's story is the beginning of the book, as Peter Dunn put it, since the story is told retrospectively by the reformed criminal, who intersperses moralizing reflections in his narrative of events.[17] But critics debate how to understand Guzmán's eventual redemption. Those who see the early picaresque novels mainly as social commentary and entertainment in the face of unsettling poverty and social unrest in Spain are inclined to dismiss the moral and religious dimension and regard Guzmán's redemption as ambiguous or an afterthought, at least for the presumed readers of the book. Michel Cavillac, who has spent much of his scholarly life probing the depths of this novel, which he regards as the great underappreciated literary work of Golden Age Spain, sees the moral dimension as fundamental to the novel's purpose, not an afterthought or routine filler.[18] To Cavillac, the novel is in good part a Christian, Counter-Reformation allegory wrapped in a picaresque-adventure package—a fateful journey into the world of original sin and the particular corruptions of the time and place, a journey of penitence that opens out to a final redemption. The novel becomes, as Alemán himself put it, a kind of *atalaya*—a watchtower onto the soul, surveying the forest as well as individual trees of the human comedy.[19]

El buscón

The third celebrated early novel in a picaresque vein is *La vida del buscón, llamado Don Pablos* (The Life of the Grifter Don Pablos), by one of Spain's literary lions in the early seventeenth century, Francisco de Quevedo. Probably written before 1610, soon after the second part of *Guzmán de Alfarache* appeared, it seems to gesture toward both *Lazarillo de Tormes* and *Guzmán de Alfarache*. The protagonist, Pablos, attended the University of Alcalá, as Guzmán had, and Pablos the aspiring gentleman conspicuously picks his teeth in public, as if he had just eaten, as Lazarillo's penurious squire does, in order to hide his hunger. *La vida del buscón* was a best seller when it was first published in 1626, with at least nine printings by 1631, but few editions appeared later in the seventeenth and eighteenth centuries.[20]

Quevedo's novel has many of the features that distinguish early picaresque works: the first-person narrative of a poor boy of doubtful origin setting out to make his way in the world, unhealthily obsessed with honor, shame, and pretensions to the standing of an *hidalgo*—a person of worth, with Christian warriors and proprietors in the family tree, a noble in waiting entitled to deference and the prospect of exemption from the taxes paid by commoners. Even with the early support of a distinguished patron and some university education, he is soon disabused of the idea that he could become a gentleman of means and leisure, an honored *hidalgo*, by his talents and pretensions alone. Most of the motley characters he meets in his travels from Segovia to Alcalá, back to Segovia, and on to Madrid, Toledo, and Sevilla cheat him mercilessly. He quickly hones his own talent for cheating, reneging on promises, and swindling the innocent as well as his abusers. His transient companions are mostly "gentlemen of prey"[21] in the underworld of burgeoning cities in Castile—rascals with nicknames like Gaptooth and Snatch-Claw. All seek to live and satisfy their appetites by taking what is not theirs, lying, and posing as beggars, gentlemen, and uniformed professionals, although only Pablos dares to disguise himself briefly as a Benedictine monk. But in the life of this *pícaro* there is no room for religion or religious scruples. As Pablos puts it in a rare reference to religion, "As a lad I always hung out around churches, and it sure wasn't because I'm such a good Christian."[22] The one clergyman in the novel is a Rabelaisian hermit monk who fleeces Pablos and his companions at cards and then wolfs down sixty eggs. No one can be trusted: his supposed friends are just friends of his money, two of whom steal the nest egg he scrapes together in his single-minded pursuit of a gentleman's standing. Always playing a role, Pablos seems most at home with a troupe of actors he meets outside Toledo, but that association, too, does not last long.

Written with Quevedo's wicked sarcasm, some of Pablos's misadventures can seem as much vehicles for strings of acrobatic quips as they are incidents that move the protagonist's life story along. And there is no resolution to Pablos's story, no comfortable—if demeaning—outcome like Lazarillo's, no resounding redemption like Guzmán's. Pablos is among the least appealing of these early picaresque characters. He is contemptuous of his relatives, mocks his victims, and is an inveterate liar and swindler who veers from derisive laughter to rage, the epitome of vengeful insolence. He is not above flattering a cloistered nun with insincere compliments and promises, and then stealing from her. He shows a glimmer of compassion only for an *hidalgo* brought low. By the end of the novel, he is physically disfigured and trapped in a life of violent crime. Yet he is a survivor. On the last page he is about to exit the scene with a new found prostitute girlfriend on a ship bound for the Indies.[23]

Estebanillo González and Others

La vida y hechos de Estebanillo González, hombre de buen humor, compuesta por él mismo published in 1646, has been considered the last representative Spanish picaresque novel in a genre that had lost its moral weight.[24] It is couched as an autobiographical memoir; the historical Estebanillo González may well have followed the path outlined in the book, but it is probably a fictionalized biography embellished for the readers' amusement by someone in the circle of the general whom Estebanillo served in Flanders during the 1640s. Whether the author is González or someone else, he is clearly aware of earlier picaresque novels, mentioning several in passing.

Estebanillo has much of the picaresque about him early in his career, when he leads a life of precarious freedom and survival free of moral scruples. While he is not born into poverty—his father was an *hidalgo* and a minor court painter in Rome—he proves to be a reckless young prankster. Apprenticed to a barber after his father's death, he flees the city a step ahead of an irate customer whose fine mustache he has mutilated. Like other *pícaros*, he is without a settled occupation or loyalties, escaping one predicament after another, always on the lookout for the next opportunity. Like a leaf tossed in the seemingly endless storm of the Thirty Years' War (1630-60), he shows up in Siena, Naples, Milan, Spain, Flanders, Germany, Poland, and the Russian Empire, always making a fool of himself by his cowardice and frivolity. He is a kitchen boy on an expedition against Turkish pirates, a camp follower and serial deserter with Spanish armies, a gambler, a fake surgeon, a peddler, a member of a gang of robbers, a day laborer, and then a servant to several dignitaries. Along the way he swindles a succession of masters and barely escapes execution for killing a man during a fight.

He is an ignominious survivor, eventually surrendering his precarious freedom and near starvation for the more comfortable humiliation of serving as court buffoon to the Imperial Commander, the Duke of Amalfi, and later to the Spanish governor of the Low Countries. Ever smiling and joking, he is regarded by his military masters and their staffs as a ridiculous, untamed animal. One of them even suggests that Estebanillo's random high spirits be "tamed" by castration, and the operation very nearly takes place.

His master muses that castration might improve Estebanillo's job prospects—as a palace guard for the women of a princely household, say, or a choir boy in a royal chapel, or a sultan's personal attendant. The arc of his life, unlike those of many early literary *pícaros*, lacks even a glimmer of possible redemption. Perhaps worse, this tale set during a devastating European war without borders is chillingly empty of any feeling for its horrors and chaos. Estebanillo is always on to the next wisecrack, the next pratfall. He believes in nothing but his own survival, scoffing at the very idea of spiritual salvation. As a helpless, crippled adult of thirty-eight, he wishes for nothing more than to retire to a bordello and gambling house in Naples, a step below even Lazarillo's inglorious but comfortable enough retirement as a cuckolded retainer.

Estebanillo's sorry tale has been taken by several scholars to mean that the picaresque genre in Spain had run its course, emptied of compassion and any tension between the *pícaro*'s isolation and even a glancing relationship to society. The author's purpose, as he says in the preface, is to amuse his noble readership, nothing more.[25] How the early Spanish picaresque novels were read, especially after the publication of *Estebanillo*, has been debated, but with little evidence of actual readers. Anne Cruz believes they were read by the mid-seventeenth century the way *Estebanillo* was purposely written—

as a string of entertaining adventures, the more scandalous the better—as if readers disregarded the Counter-Reformation moral agenda and the troubling social facts of vagrancy and poverty that gave rise to picaresque novels in the first place. José Antonio Maravall sees the early novels less as expressing elite ideology and interests and more as an indictment of social injustices that would have appealed to the poor and betrayed.[26]

For whatever reasons, *Guzmán de Alfarache* and *Lazarillo de Tormes* continued to strike a chord among readers. New editions were published, used copies circulated, and translations into German, French, and English inspired novels with a narrative line and seriousness that echoed Guzmán more than Estebanillo.[27] Two of the most popular new novels had in mind a moral purpose for telling stories about picaresque vagabonds. H.J.C. von Grimmelshausen's *The Adventures of Simplicius Simplicissimus* is the best-known German example. First published in 1668/1669, *Simplicius* is also set in the Thirty Years' War, but with a very different vagabond protagonist and a different trajectory in the end. In both cases, an inexperienced, in some ways innocent boy is propelled into a chaotic, corrupted world and learns to survive in devious and expedient ways—lying, cheating, impersonating, swindling. There are betrayals and narrow escapes on the battlefield and elsewhere, but unlike Estebanillo, Simplicius is no coward or idler. Nor is he stripped of his humanity. He still recognizes suffering and exploitation, and is capable of affection and remorse. He begins to lament his lost innocence and regrets his many sins, but does nothing to atone for them until eventually he accompanies an acquaintance on a pilgrimage to a regional shrine and discovers what to him seems an earthly paradise of happy, healthy, well-fed people living without fear of being cheated, betrayed, or plundered. He soon leaves the chaotic world of war and sin to live alone on an island as a penitent hermit, commending himself to God for protection, making the island into a pleasure garden, and praising his merciful God for "thus far preserving me from everlasting damnation, . . . giving me time and opportunity to better myself, . . . to beg His forgiveness and to thank Him and His mercies."[28]

Simplicius Simplicissimus enjoyed instant success, going through five editions by 1674, but its Baroque religious overtones were less appealing to eighteenth-century readers,[29] whereas Alain-René Lesage's multivolume classic French picaresque novel, *Gil Blas*, was a best seller in several languages.[30] *The Adventures of Gil Blas of Santillana* is set in mid-seventeenth-century Spain, perhaps as a nod to the quintessential Spanishness of the genre, but written and published later, in three parts, in 1715, 1724, and 1735. The author knew every line of *Guzmán de Alfarache*, having published his own translation, and *Gil Blas* shares some similarities in narrative structure with the Spanish novel. There is the inexperienced but talented young protagonist of modest means, on the road, seeking freedom and fortune, but thrown off course by early encounters with robbers, liars, and cheats. Stumbling along the way as he travels widely, Gil Blas meets an array of people and learns the tricks of various trades. But his better self begins to emerge earlier than it does for Guzmán and he enters the road toward redemption as an honest, resourceful, and upstanding citizen. The strongest similarity to *Guzmán de Alfarache* is Lesage's insistence on his moral messaging. In his preface, the author-protagonist emphasizes that his purpose in writing is not just to spin entertaining stories; it is also to instruct. But this is picaresque literature modulated from a Counter-Reformation key to a radiantly secular French Enlightenment one. Love, loyalty, honesty, and friendship win the day. Unlike Estebanillo and Guzmán, Gil Blas is a good person at heart from the beginning, although Guzmán's words could easily have been his: "I think all men are like me, weak, easily led, with their natural passions."[31] He displays the full range of human emotions—contempt, compassion, despair, vanity, arrogance, love, friendship, generosity, joy, and grief—though for a time his heart is made "harder than flint" by ambition and rivalries, and an appetite for luxuries. But there are good people and goodness in the world, too. Gil Blas is a networker, earning by his loyalty, diligence, and courage the trust of various estimable masters high on the social and political ladder, all the way up to the Count-Duke of Olivares, the royal favorite of Philip IV. By the end of the saga, Gil Blas has been knighted and is happily married to the beautiful young Dorothea. He has carved out a personal heaven on earth, much as Fernández de Lizardi's Periquillo does in more modest circumstances (more on this shortly).

There is general agreement across the trenches of scholarship that these novels present *pícaro* protagonists, as various as they may have been. They are known mainly as undefined and unsettled characters of many faces in their orphan-like freedom, if not estrangement from society. But they are not altogether apart. They spend their lives among people often pretending to be someone else, becoming what they need to be in order to cheat death and make their way in the world. Ambiguous outsiders, often with outsize appetites, they lack steady loyalties or employment. They are small-time swindlers, thieves more than robbers, usually with some education, clever persuaders, and shameless impostors. Diego de Torres Villarroel, a widely published eighteenth-century Spanish author and professor of mathematics at the University of Salamanca who thought of himself as a *pícaro* in his youth and evidently admired picaresque rebelliousness while deploring "the stupidities and derangement of my liberty, laziness, and presumption," suggested that one more characteristic was essential: insolence.[32] Others suggest that early literary *pícaros* are best described as vagabonds trying to stay a step ahead of poverty and the law.

Pícaros have also been described as tricksters, or the offspring of mythic tricksters.[33] Like *pícaros*, tricksters are wandering strangers and agents of disorder, and they are protean characters operating with an unsettling freedom.[34] They dupe and are duped. They are survivors, if not always winners. Like *pícaros*, they are selfish loners, and at the mercy of unruly appetites, yet appealing in their way. When they win, they win with ingenuity and honeyed words more than brute strength. But I hesitate to call *pícaros* "tricksters" because that would blunt a fundamental difference: tricksters are not just disguised but true shape-shifters, legendary characters and collective personifications beyond time and place. They have a dual nature: animal and human, primitive and civilized. They may steal fire and light for the people, but they are also responsible for human mortality. They can see into the heart of things, and they sow disorder and change on a grander scale than could a merely human social orphan.

It is true that the *pícaro* usually poses as more than an ordinary criminal. With freewheeling ambition, he revels in his performance as an impostor, but his cause is his own survival and pleasure. Tricksters, Lewis Hyde proposes, deceive and steal not so much to get rich "as to disturb the established categories of truth and property, and, by so doing, open the road to possible new worlds."[35] In contrast, the key to the "life" of a *pícaro*, as these early Spanish novels put it in their titles, is *personal* change, a learning process that usually begins with a crisis. The protagonist passes from innocence and want to alienation, delinquency, betrayal, revenge, and—possibly—redemption, a journey best exemplified by Guzmán de Alfarache and Simplicius, although even Pablos recognizes that redemption would require change.[36]

While the terms are not synonyms, considering the role of tricksters in folklore raises unresolved questions that can be asked about literary *pícaros* as well. Were trickster stories an expression of oppressed groups trying to make their way in a hostile world, a criticism of society and politics as they are? Or did they express privileged groups' anxieties about maintaining order? Where did trickster stories circulate? Did legendary tricksters inspire some wayward adolescents to strike out on their own as cocksure delinquents and aspiring idlers? Did shamans in eighteenth-century Mexico understand themselves to be trickster heroes? That is, in Alexander Blackburn's words, were trickster stories the "deep down myth" for picaresque literature? Or is it likely that stories of wily tricksters sprang from local history more often than from an established literary or folkloric tradition, as Enrique Lamadrid proposes for coyote trickster stories that circulate by word of mouth in northern New Mexico communities?[37] Or is there a feedback loop at play, in which legendary rascals inspire local behavior that in turn leads to new or embellished stories? *Pícaros* may be tricksters in the making if they are remembered and embraced, but they remain only too human, whether in literary form or rising from the pages of historical records.

Mexican Literary Pícaros?

If Javier Treviño Castro is right that "in Mexico the picaresque is alive every day, as if this was its birthplace," it is odd that so few works of picaresque fiction originated there during the colonial period.[38] And whether the few written before Mexico's Revolution of 1910 have much in common with the classic Hispanic novels is debatable. Three contenders are usually mentioned: *Infortunios de Alonso Ramírez* (1690), written by New Spain's celebrated polymath Carlos de Sigüenza y Góngora, and two works by José Joaquín Fernández de Lizardi, *El Periquillo Sarniento* (1816) and *Vida y hechos del famoso caballero Don Catrín de la Fachenda* (1820).[39]

Alonso Ramírez in Sigüenza's account of his "misfortunes" has been called picaresque, and as a historical character he may well have identified with the early struggles of literary *pícaros* and been something of a fabulist, but judging by the text itself he seems to have had little in common with the cunning and shameless ways of the Spanish *pícaros*—or with Aguayo or Atondo. The illiterate son of a poor ship's carpenter in Puerto Rico, Ramírez leaves home at thirteen to make his fortune, *para ser rico*. This beginning sounds like it has the makings of a picaresque tale of an innocent outcast in a corrupt world; and indeed, like the classic picaresque novels, *Infortunios* is a first-person, episodic narrative of a young man on the margins of society who encounters an array of lowlife characters along the way. After several failed attempts to catch on as a carpenter in Puebla and Mexico City, a rebuff by a prosperous relative of his mother living in the Chontal region of Oaxaca in southern Mexico, and suffering the heartbreaking death of his virtuous young wife, the despairing young man takes ship in 1682 for the Philippines, where he becomes a skilled seaman. He is captured by English pirates and later enslaved by buccaneers, who hold him for three years before finally casting him adrift on the coast of Madagascar. Somehow he and his companions manage to cross the Atlantic. After running aground on the coast of Yucatán, he walks inland and eventually reached Mexico City. There, in 1689, he meets with a viceroy who passes him on to Sigüenza to have his story told in writing. Sigüenza's text, with Ramírez as the putative narrator, was published the following year.

But despite their shared will to live—Ramírez declares that "I endured all these things because of my love of life"[40]—Ramírez seems to be a very different character from Lazarillo de Tormes, Guzmán de Alfarache, or Quevedo's Pablos, perhaps too good to be true. His aim, he says, was not to seek adventure for its own sake, but to get ahead by working hard, to settle into family life, and to honor his God and king. Indeed, he comes across as a paragon of integrity, piety, courage, and loyalty. His harrowing adventures display none of the small-time subversions of authority, none of the biting humor, selfish appetites, lies, deceptions, and impersonations we expect from a *pícaro*. Accordingly, *Infortunios de Alonso Ramírez* has attracted more attention from students of picaresque literature for its literary conventions and episodic narrative structure than for the character of its protagonist. The main question has been whether to consider it a *ficción*—largely a fictional product of Sigüenza's making and imagination—or a *relación*, akin to a *relación de méritos y servicios* or personal résumé—a factual, if selective, account of extraordinary achievements and services, written both to entertain and to appeal for favor from the king or his agents.[41] The *Infortunios* pointedly declares Ramirez's loyalty to the Spanish Empire, the Church, and the king—in whose largesse, Sigüenza declares, Ramírez has reason to expect a share.[42]

Of course, *ficción* and *relación* are not mutually exclusive as narrative types. Historical accounts, whether by participants or later historians, are partly fictions, too, selecting and framing facts to tell a plausible, coherent story, with a point of view. They are not unedited replays of events from every possible vantage point. The use of words, in itself, makes a historical account a condensed, selective translation.[43] And Sigüenza surely produced something other than a verbatim transcription of what Ramírez told him. The attention to geography, natural resources, navigation, and patterns of trade may well have been Sigüenza's contribution even if most or all of the details were elicited from Ramírez. It was certainly the kind of inside information about the Far East that both informant and writer would have recognized as valuable to the king and might earn his favor. How much of *Infortunios* is Sigüenza's voice and story, and how much is Ramírez's truth and lies?[44] It is impossible to say for sure, and most scholars have been content to describe it as both, in some measure: "a text that must be celebrated for its ambiguity."[45] Substantial new research points emphatically both away from and toward *Infortunios* as Sigüenza's creation and a *ficción* more of Ramírez's making. As background research by Fabio López Lázaro shows, it was understood at the time as a *relación*—no doubt embellished for effect—of a living man's experiences promoted by a viceroy for his political purposes. And in an ambitious essay, José F. Buscaglia-Salgado suggests that the historical Ramírez was no mere upright citizen or *pícaro*, but "a consummate impostor who, as a modern-colonial subject, had grown to become a true master of the confidence trick."[46]

Fernández de Lizardi's *El Periquillo Sarniento* is not universally regarded as a picaresque novel despite the similarities in its narrative form and the character of the protagonist (whom the author sometimes calls a *pícaro*) to early Spanish examples, especially *Guzmán de Alfarache*. The story of young libertine Periquillo is told episodically, in the first person until the last chapter, after Periquillo dies. Dozens of characters populate the story as he moves around, most of them from society's seedy lower reaches. As in *Guzmán de Alfarache*, there are many moralizing asides and much derisive humor in *Periquillo Sarniento*—Fernández de Lizardi, like Alemán, says he means to instruct as well as entertain. And like his literary predecessors, his protagonist is a young delinquent in a merciless, turbulent world.

Through much of the novel, Periquillo is a wisecracking hustler-predator, captive to his appetites. He is a survivor, although sometimes his own enemy when things are going well. He is a quick study in the arts of deception, a performer who becomes what he needs to be at the moment, a practiced liar who betrays and is betrayed. Then near the end, in a remarkable reversal much like that of Guzmán de Alfarache, he is marvelously redeemed, becoming a faithful companion, family man, upright citizen, and friend of worthy priests and Catholic rites.

Young Periquillo's rudderless drift toward idle pleasure at the expense of others in and near Mexico City leads through university halls, gambling dens, theology study, marriage, and the mean streets and jails of the capital. He squanders a meager inheritance; his first wife dies in poverty, neglected by her husband; he is briefly apprenticed to a scribe, a barber-surgeon, and a pharmacist; he poses as a physician in Tula and is run out of town when his quackery causes needless deaths during an epidemic; he becomes a sexton's helper—all the time pretending to be what he is not, trading on phony erudition and empty promises. He squanders his luckiest break as interim district governor of Tixtla. In Fernández de Lizardi's version of absolute power corrupting absolutely, Periquillo admits that he "got up to my old tricks" during the few weeks he had the unchecked powers of a governor:

To start off, I banished a pretty girl from the town because she lived in debauchery. That's what was said; but the true reason was that she refused to go along with my solicitations. . . . After that, with the help of a tiny gift of 300 pesos, I incriminated a poor man whose only crime was to be married to a beautiful, dishonorable woman. . . . Next I hunted down and threatened all the other poor men who were guilty of the same crime, and they, fearful that I might banish their mistresses as I was wont to do, paid me whatever fines I demanded. Nor did I neglect to revoke the most properly drawn-up documents. . . . To top it all off, I set up public gaming sessions in the government offices. . . . One night they took me for so much money that I didn't have a penny of my own, so I unlocked the community chest and gambled away all the money it held.[47]

Sentenced to eight years of militia service in the Philippines, Periquillo wheedles his way into a comfortable desk job as the colonel's adjutant, where he has the opportunity to show off his fine penmanship. He returns to Mexico unreformed and unabashed, now posing as a rich count. He falls in with a gang of thieves near Mexico City at the Río Frío pass, is unsettled by the sight of a hanged man, and resolves—not for the first time—to reform. But this time he attends a spiritual retreat in preparation for making a general confession, and the priest-confessor turns out to be his childhood friend and fellow delinquent Martín Pelayo, no longer "a dancing and scatterbrained boy, but a wise, exemplary and circumspect priest."[48] Periquillo makes a heartfelt confession, and the compassionate Father Pelayo arranges honest work for him as manager of an inn near Mexico City. Overcome with gratitude,

Periquillo becomes a model employee, charitable citizen, and eventually the innkeeper. He rescues and marries the daughter of another old, true friend, Don Antonio, and lives out a virtuous life of marital bliss.

Those who do not regard *Periquillo Sarniento* as a picaresque novel by a sixteenth- or seventeenth-century European standard note that Fernández de Lizardi's moral lessons, unlike those of the earlier novels, are not rooted in a theology of original sin.[49] Rather, the author is seen as a child of the Enlightenment, interested in the perfectibility of humankind through educational reforms and useful knowledge, and the enemy of entrenched attitudes about hereditary privilege and authority that scorn honest work and civic and personal virtue.[50] The hand of Jean-Jacques Rousseau, the great outsider, is apparent in Periquillo's resounding moral transformation, and in the theme of friendship that runs throughout the story, first as allegiance and regard taken for granted or betrayed by Periquillo and toward the end as friendship of an unqualified kind that Periquillo gives and receives: "I am your friend, and that's what I'll always be so long as you honor me with your friendship," and "there are lots of friends, but few friendships. Friends swarm like flies when the weather's nice, but few remain when it turns bad."[51] Here are echoes of Rousseau's view that people generally are good, but morality and virtue must be nurtured by rational education and example. Morality and virtue are expressed above all in true and selfless friendship, which, without proper education, is undermined by jealousy and fear.

Fernández de Lizardi's affinity for Rousseau and the Age of Reason is not in doubt, but leaving Catholicism and picaresque predecessors out of his moral vision empties the novel of its religious dimension. He does not mention Guzmán de Alfarache or other early works, but his novel is structured in much the same way—as a first-person narrative of picaresque episodes with a righteous conversion at the end—and José Mariano Beristáin de Souza (1756–1817), creole canon in the cathedral of the Archdiocese of Mexico, public intellectual, and bibliographer who celebrated the intellectual achievements of Spanish Americans, recognized a remarkable similarity between Guzmán and Fernández de Lizardi's Periquillo.[52] Fernández de Lizardi does not share a theological horizon grounded in original sin, but neither does he echo Rousseau's sweeping denunciation of the clergy, nor dismiss religion, nor satirize it as barren and mendacious solemnity. Instead, he occasionally turns to biblical moralizing, as do Guzmán de Alfarache and Simplicius Simplicissimus. Periquillo invokes the Psalms to recommend the joys of worship: "The righteous—in the words of holy King David—should rejoice and be glad in the Lord," and he praises the consolation of belief and religious ritual: "Your mother was inconsolable with this loss, and had to take advantage of all the considerations with which the Catholic religion alleviates us in such situations, for it can minister sound comforts to the truly bereaved."[53] Mass and confession are an essential part of Periquillo's transformation and good death, including his hymn to the Supreme Being.[54]

More often than not, Fernández de Lizardi's priests are men of good will and compassion. The parish priest of Tixtla is a grasping despot, the tormentor of his flock,[55] but his counterpart in Tula is a staunch protector of the Indians in his parish, and the good priest of Chilapa is "virtuous without a trace of hypocrisy." And of course, near the end of the novel Periquillo's boyhood friend Martín Pelayo, now a model priest, hears Periquillo's heartfelt confession and comes to administer the last rites and offer the consolation of companionship in the hour of his death.[56]

Were Rousseau and Father Pelayo strange bedfellows for Fernández de Lizardi and his early readers? Not really. In *El Periquillo Sarniento* the moral foundation of a just society is not a choice between religion and Enlightenment humanism. It is both, together. Late in the novel, after Periquillo's redemption, he and his bookkeeper come upon a misanthrope, badly injured in a fall from his horse, who threatens them with a pistol. Periquillo declares, "It would not be right at all to leave him in this state. Humanity and religion demand that we help him. Let's do it." Then at the end of the novel Periquillo urges his children to "love and honor God and observe His precepts."⁵⁷

Fernández de Lizardi's novella published four years later, *Vida y hechos del famoso caballero Don Catrín de la Fachenda* (Mr. Dandy Show-Off) offers a narrower, more heavy-handed and acerbic indictment of "the neglect and desolation" visited upon Mexico by the privileged classes of Spanish rule. Here we have the author as secular reformer, child of the Enlightenment, apparently leaving religion aside. He roundly denounces the useless, preening Don Catrín, but does not exactly blame him for his worst failings. Instead, the fault lies with inept and overindulgent parents, a deficient system of education, the bad example of self-serving elites, and disdain for work ingrained in the culture.

Unlike most literary *pícaros* before him, Catrín is a pampered, conceited, cowardly dandy, not an impoverished social orphan. In spite of his formal education and measure of talent, he is a lazy, unenlightened windbag, a delicate flower with few survival skills. But like the literary *pícaros* before him, he avoids honest work whenever possible, sheds friends without a second thought, lies, cheats, and pretends to be what he is not. He is too self-absorbed to be a sly or very resourceful cheater, but will stoop to a swindle when the need and opportunity arise—as when he tricks a "simpleton" out of a string of pearls by pretending to be buying them as an agent for the provincial of a convent.[58] But grifting and theft rarely go well for Catrín. Arrested in a failed scheme to steal a large sum of money from an elderly merchant, he is sent to Havana for two years' penal servitude. He returns home unchastened, vowing never again to work, and to devote himself only to pleasure and "get by on my own without shame."[59] Still a young man, he ends up a beggar and a penniless wreck. After a sham confession, he dies at thirty-one, unrepentant, convinced that dandies like himself are "honorable men, honest men and, above all, noble gentlemen."[60] Fernández de Lizardi sums it up: "He lived badly and died the same way."[61]

Conclusion

However they are described, Early Modern European picaresque novels beginning with *Lazarillo de Tormes* were a striking departure from the long-popular romances of chivalry and pastoral novels. Most often navigating a bleak world of original sin, they (and *El Periquillo Sarniento* in the early nineteenth century) take readers on a journey to the edges of an unsettled social order, into a world of appearances where a code of honor might be invoked, but hardly applied. Presented as fractured mirrors of their societies, they reflected tensions and anxieties of the time, especially about simulation, veiled intentions, imposture, deceit, and displacement. They often mixed episodes of action, suspense, biting humor, and grief in a moral satire, warning of grave threats to public order and salvation expressed in thoughts and actions of picaresque characters that undermine those objectives. The same kind of official anxiety about disorder and determination to regulate was expressed in colonial sumptuary laws and in the solemn Corpus Christi processions of well-ordered ranks of dignitaries and sacred images, with prancing buffoons and a grotesque *tarasca* figure—the fearsome dragon-fish with a lion's head that was tamed by Saint Martha—bringing up the rear, rendering visible the ever-present threat to celestial and civic order from Satan and his minions. Guzmán de Alfarache, Simplicius, Gil Blas, and even Quevedo's Pablos conveyed a moral message that focused on personal redemption as a solution to social disorder, and how difficult it is to achieve. Fernández de Lizardi's moralizing was more hopeful about reform and redemption, in the spirit of Rousseau, but without Rousseau's animus toward religion. Despite the wickedness in Periquillo's world, ordinary people are basically good, and goodness can win out with resolve, education, true friendship, and moral principles, including those grounded in religion.

The classic early picaresque novels and their protagonists were known to readers and a wider public in eighteenth-century Spain and Spanish America, but how they were received in their time and later is not so clear. From one perspective, by the time *La vida y hechos de Estebanillo González* was published in 1646, the moral messages of the picaresque were lost on consumers who just wanted a good laugh at someone else's expense. Literary *pícaros* were reduced to buffoons, or they were read the way governors, merchants, and other people of privilege might have looked upon real vagabonds and grifters—as dangerous, disorderly characters who needed to be controlled or denied and removed. But is a blend of escapist entertainment and social control enough to explain the longevity and wide reach of *Lazarillo de Tormes*, *Guzmán de Alfarache*, *Simplicius Simplicissimus*, and some other early examples of picaresque fiction? *Was* the moral critique and rebelliousness in them largely ignored by consumers after the mid-seventeenth century? Speculating about readers and rumors without direct evidence is just that: speculation. But how can the continuing popularity of some of those early picaresque novels—especially *Guzmán de Alfarache* in New Spain—be explained? If the exploits of Guzmán *el pícaro* were known by ordinary people, was he regarded as a sort of hero, or at least an antihero along the lines of the durable but luckless Wile E. Coyote in his role as foil to Roadrunner's cheerful (meep, meep) invincibility? Did they vicariously savor the way *pícaros* they had heard of, or perhaps known, lived? That is, did the circulation of stories from these books in Spain and New Spain long after they were first published suggest identification with the *pícaros'* habit of tempting fate and living to tell the tale, their improvisations, their quick wit? If so, were consumers thumbing their noses at the established order of things—the elites' assumption that common people were a stain on the social and moral order and that *pícaros* and *vagabundos* were a criminal caste or mad?⁶² Seventeenth- and eighteenth-century people in Spain and New Spain had learned from their own experience, and perhaps from authors like Baltasar Gracián, to be wary of appearances, including their own. Don't trust your friends completely, warned Gracián. They could become your enemies. And, sinners, beware of your inner *pícaro*.

4 Aguayo and Atondo, Pícaros After All?

*"Pablos, open your eyes! There's meat on the grill and you have to look out
for yourself because there is no other mother or father here for you."*[1]

As young men, Joseph Aguayo and Juan Atondo seemed to lead
picaresque lives in an almost literary way. They were born poor, but
not destitute. Both were on their own as young delinquents disowned by family, without steadfast friends or community ties, living on deception and broken promises. Like Lazarillo de Tormes,
Guzmán de Alfarache, and Periquillo, they were protean figures
and on the move—Aguayo wandering the roads and hill towns of
the Bajío area north of Mexico City, perfecting his impersonations;
Atondo dithering over the prospect of a friar's life, fleeing a shotgun
marriage, deserting the military, and more. Poverty shadowed their
lives, but it did not define them. Both had several years of schooling
and, as putative Old Christians of Spanish descent—"descendants
of Heaven," as Francisco de Quevedo put it[2]—they felt entitled to
deference and service, perhaps imagining a time when they would
prove their God-given nobility. They avoided manual labor when
they could and padded their claims to professional standing. In
their way, they were players in the colonial drama, albeit self-

marginalizing. Even in impersonating priests, neither regarded himself as an apostate. As neo-*pícaros*, Aguayo and Atondo were selfish survivors, preying on others to satisfy their own appetites, neither tragic nor simply repugnant. They reneged on promises and betrayed trust, and their indifference toward women is chilling, but as far as I can tell they were not violent or involved in an assault on the order of things, and their risky, sometimes slapstick escapades must have made for entertaining local gossip.

Aguayo

"The pícaro both incorporates and transcends the wanderer, the jester, and the have-not."

—CLAUDIO GUILLÉN[3]

José Joaquín Fernández de Lizardi would not have been surprised that Aguayo reminded me of his Periquillo Sarniento. More than once Periquillo tells the reader that he knew many men like himself:

> If every man would present the public his life story written with as much simplicity and precision as mine, you would find a multitude of Periquillos in the world: their ups and downs, their favorable and adverse adventures are only hidden from our view because each of them endeavors to conceal his indiscretions.[4]

Much about Aguayo's life story from childhood to his last recorded brush with the Inquisition echoes the early years of several of the Spanish literary *pícaros* and Fernández de Lizardi's Periquillo. Aguayo, too, was a runaway propelled by poverty and an ambition to escape his circumstances, to seek his "libertad" (freedom) and prove himself, but without too much effort. Part of the mystique of *pícaros* in literature and life is that they are like corks in a turbulent stream, going where the current takes them, and no matter the trouble, they keep bobbing back to the surface, soaking wet but not much the worse for wear.

Poverty, delinquency, cunning, and literacy were the main ingredients of Aguayo's picaresque self, as they were to varying degrees for the literary *pícaros*. Positing a literate protagonist allowed the authors to narrate selectively what they understood the audience wanted or needed to hear, just as Aguayo crafted stories to tell the Inquisition what would be advantageous to him. Aguayo was selective in what he said about his past, rarely showing his emotions in an unguarded way, as he did in his first trial when he blamed his father for his delinquency. Later, when he admitted guilt, it was in delphic terms, withholding most of the incriminating details, especially about his years in Cuba.

Think of other familiar traits of literary *pícaros*, and most of them apply to Aguayo: vagabond; thief, but not vicious; liar and cheater at the expense of credulous people; gambler; impostor; idler; disguising his poverty, or exposing it extravagantly as a beggar or threadbare traveler; sly; and well-spoken. Aguayo and the literary *pícaros* lack a moral compass or enduring loyalties. Everything is situational. They love no one and can't be trusted. He and they bear comparison to the brazen Arnaud du Tilh, the sixteenth-century French peasant who for several years succeeded in impersonating the long-absent Martin Guerre in Guerre's home village—taking up married life with Guerre's wife and gaining the trust of Guerre's relatives and neighbors. Du Tilh, like Aguayo and the literary *pícaros*, was "fluent of tongue and had a memory an actor would envy."[5]

Aguayo was less sociable and not so obviously a social climber as Guzmán de Alfarache and Pablos, but, like them, he cared about status, and his tenuous claim to come from a line of Old Christians echoes their pretensions to privilege and a distinguished family tree—if not rising to the level of Sancho Panza's boast that "I am an Old Christian, and that alone is enough for me to be a count"[6]— which foreign observers of the time considered characteristic of Castilians.

For example, Francesco Guicciardini, the Florentine statesman and historian at the court of the King of Aragón in the early sixteenth century, attributed limited development of industry and commerce there to "the fact that the artisans have pretensions to nobility and prefer to dedicate themselves to war."[7] According to Américo Castro, roughly one in nine Castilian and Leonese families in 1541 claimed *hidalgo* status, and Ignacio Atienza Hernández documented a growing appetite for the more exalted titles of Spanish nobility throughout the sixteenth and seventeenth centuries, from 60 grandee titles in 1520, to 124 in 1597, to 241 in 1631, to 533 in 1700.[8]

Whether American conquests and colonization revived and perpetuated "the ancient ideals" of the *hidalgo* as part of Spaniards' "vital dwelling place," as scholars of an earlier generation proposed,[9] Aguayo and early literary *pícaros* seemed to embrace its core values and privileges: forgoing a life of manual labor when they could, embracing the kind of individualism expressed in the idea of the *hombre a secas* (on his own, beholden to no one but his God, himself, and his king),[10] and a conviction that they, like their real or imagined ancestors, were capable of heroic deeds and deserving of royal favor. Like Pablos, Aguayo would learn through the floggings he suffered and other mishaps and humiliations that he had no claim on even the lowliest noble standing, and could enjoy the pleasures of *hidalguía* only by deception, and then not for long. His favorite deception was to pose as a dignitary—a priest or occasionally a royal official known by his attire, bearing, and manner of speaking—in order to bask in public recognition, respect, and comforts of the home he never had. As he demonstrated while on the run at Texmelucan, Tlaxcala, the cassock, cane, and breviary were his Diner's Club card to free lodging, meals, and conviviality in the local rectory. While he was effectively homeless, unlike the literary *pícaros* he gravitated back to his hometown, the mining center of Guanajuato, several times. He was not there to look up relatives and friends. Fernández de Lizardi would have sensed the reason for those visits and something of Aguayo's broader outlook in his opinion that Mexico's great silver mines largely explained why Mexico was plagued with vagabonds and erstwhile *hidalgos*. He has one of Periquillo's patrons comment that countries have been made poor and debased by the easy wealth of silver mines, producing lazy opportunists who "sponge off an accidental fortune," never learn a trade or other respectable occupation, and produce nothing of value themselves: "Everyone knows that mining people are generally depraved, provocative, arrogant and wasteful."[11]

Two differences between Aguayo and the most familiar picaresque story are especially striking. In Aguayo's case, there is no redemption, no happy return to the fold. And it appears that Aguayo was more the loner than were any of the literary *pícaros*, with their communities of fellow thieves and successions of masters and wives or lovers. Aguayo made a point of claiming he lived and acted alone and had no masters who favored him along the way. If so, we might ask how it was that he gained an early release from his incarceration and penal servitude in the fortress of Santiago, Cuba. Had he played up to the commander there? And how did he become a ship's clerk early in his time in Cuba, eluding, like Periquillo, the backbreaking presidio work he had every reason to expect at the end of his second Inquisition trial? Was it only because of his literacy?

For all that Aguayo revealed about himself and others observed about him in the Inquisition records, he remains an enigma compared to the literary *pícaros*. Did he associate with many different kinds of people, as the *pícaros* of fiction did? Probably, but he said he didn't and we don't hear much about them, except for a few of his jail mates. Who was Aguayo beyond the impersonations? Unlike the literary *pícaros*, who reveal some of their inner feelings, motives, and resentments, Aguayo was largely closed about his feelings and social relationships beyond a conventional display of humility and piety when required, keeping his options open to craft the next half-truth. He reveals more of himself in what he did—in less scripted moments lashing out at his father during the first trial, and his daring escapes and improvised impersonations—and in occasional incidents described by eyewitnesses in which we can glimpse the pleasure it gave him to pose as an authority, dressed in a cassock and occupying the seat of honor at a fandango, or perched above kneeling penitents who came to him for confession. For all his caginess, his theatrical gestures dared the audience to question who he was.

Pablos in Quevedo's *La vida del buscón* resembles Aguayo in a way that separates him from most other literary *pícaros*: he stayed on the road to perdition.[12] These two share some more familiar traits as charlatans: they were adroit readers of others and preyed on their innocence and inattention. They were impostors and performers who could lie without misgiving, and who gained trust in part by their appearance—Aguayo's slight and youthful physique suggested that he was harmless, while Pablos had "the face of a smart fellow with good judgment."[13] They betrayed and were betrayed; gratitude and friendship were not their way. But the differences between them are great, too. Both were practiced liars, but Aguayo was more subtle and dissimulating in his dishonesty, trading in lies that had the ring of truth, while Pablos "did not even tell the truth by accident" in his rush to fit in and "live among illustrious people and gentlemen."[14] Quevedo placed his Pablos *in* society, posing as a gentleman, hanging out in cities or with a troupe of actors, or leading a small criminal gang. Ruled more by greed, envy, and, above all, shame, Pablos aims higher than Aguayo and emerges as more repulsive, as Quevedo exaggerates his villainy to critique social mobility itself, as if trying to climb above one's God-given place is itself a lie. For example, Pablos rejects his hangman uncle who loves him unreservedly, dismissing him with a "good riddance you bugger, you're a disgrace to decent people."[15] But whether Pablos is more shameless than Aguayo, more impious and sacrilegious, more driven by money, apparel, and his animal appetites, or more cynical, we can't be sure. While Quevedo lets us in on Pablos's "real" feelings and intentions, and Mateo Alemán had Guzmán de Alfarache share his inner thoughts and how he comes to understand his own wicked motives, we have little sense from the written record whether Aguayo was introspective and anxious in this way. He remains mysterious, seemingly on the threshold of remorse and redemption, required to perform spiritual exercises, do penance, show contrition, and endure years of exile and penal servitude, but then reverting to form again and again—conning, stealing, impersonating, and plotting his next escape.

Pablos and Guzmán de Alfarache are driven by an aggrieved sense of honor and pride, imagining themselves to be worthy of recognition as *hidalgos*. Guzmán, like Pablos, is brought down by his relentless ambition to be a man of some consequence; as Peter N. Dunn explains, private humiliations lead to his thirst for revenge.[16] Honor was a luxury Aguayo could ill afford, but pride played into his sense of himself in the world, a pride that could turn to hubris when he posed as an official, and it brought him down more than once. He identified himself, and was nominally accepted in court proceedings, as a man of Spanish and Old Christian ancestry, eligible for the noble professions, including the priesthood. It must have stung that strangers he met in his guise as a priest saw him as an *indito*, an insignificant little Indian, although even that indignity could prove useful to cloak his cunning. He was evidently also proud of his ability to improvise and persuade. Whether or not the risks of impersonation and escape gave him an addict's rush, it took some nerve to seek out a district judge and complain—in high dudgeon, wearing a priest's cassock and wielding the fancy cane of an agent of the Inquisition—that his landlady had confiscated his (probably stolen) horse. Had he come to feel invulnerable, or just desperate, when he and the unsavory Augustín Solano hatched their risky plan in the Guanajuato jail to commit sham acts of sacrilege and witchcraft that would get them sent on to the Inquisition cells in Mexico City? They must have hoped that they would be released with a stern warning not to trifle with the Holy Office. But their testimony became tangled in contradictions, mutual distrust, and recriminations such that Aguayo's artful half-truths and wordsmithing were ignored. The lesson he apparently took from that debacle was not that it was time to mend his ways and atone for his sins, but that he should become even more closed and wary. Trust no one but yourself.

Atondo

"You are the stranger who gets stranger by the hour"

—JAMES TATE[17]

During his restless periods, Juan Atondo could be taken for a fitful and protean *pícaro*, with his distaste for regular employment, strings of lies, betrayals, unruly appetites, sudden urges, pretenses, and abrupt departures. In the winding, guilt-ridden saga of incidents and sins he recounted for the Inquisition, Atondo admitted to lies, then conjured up a few new ones that undermined his credibility again. Like Guzmán de Alfarache and Quevedo's Pablos, Atondo coveted fine clothes, uniforms, and ostentatious display, in the way Baltasar Gracián described his fellow Spaniards: "frugal in eating and sober in drinking, but excessive in how they dress."[18] Pablos's obsession with status and dissimulation is reflected in his fastidious attention to clothing, too. Aiming to charm a community of nuns out of their worldly possessions, he puts on "the outfit I used to wear when I played handsome young suitors in comedies,"[19] and before setting out for Toledo he extended himself to buy a sedate gray traveling suit, a collar, and a sword. Clothes were his armor, covering and protecting his vulnerability, so he was disconcerted by the bedraggled *hidalgo* he met on the way to Madrid, whose ragged cape and collar barely hid the fact that he wore no shirt underneath and was holding up his torn breeches with one hand, his buttocks exposed at the back. "You can see everything about me, since I conceal nothing," lamented the *hidalgo*.[20]

Of course, the idea that "clothes make the man"—that snap judgments about strangers' or casual acquaintances' character, status, ethnicity, occupation, and community membership can be made from their appearance—is not only Spanish. Similar sayings about the look of authority or respectability circulated in Asia and Egypt long before Gracián, and when Erasmus of Rotterdam framed the adage in Latin (*vestis virum facit*) in the early sixteenth century, he referred to Quintilian, the first-century CE Roman rhetorician: "To dress within the formal limits and with an air gives men . . . authority."[21] But in this Spanish society in Europe and overseas that set so much store in appearances and pageantry, uniforms and finery invited picaresque deceptions and impersonations as well as feeding personal vanity and prompting sumptuary laws to prevent people from dressing above their station, such as the royal laws forbidding Black women from wearing pearls or silk.

Vanity and his skill with scissors and thread may have driven Atondo's taste for stylish clothes and the theft of his wife's dresses when he deserted the family home, but it also served to make him a more presentable suitor and a more trustworthy stranger when he approached the Franciscans and later posed as a priest. Nevertheless, much about Atondo as a *pícaro* does not fit with his written confession and oral testimony. The confession is a strange document, and not only because it was a voluntary, overlong creation on his part. It is a rambling, sometimes breathless presentation that slopes off into repetition and digression, not the kind of restrained, practiced, ingratiating testimony one would expect from a *pícaro*, careful not to reveal too much while strategically admitting guilt and appealing for mercy. It is the work of an anxious man in an agitated state, at least intermittently overwhelmed by shame and remorse. Both in his words and in the testimony of others, he displayed little of the *pícaros'* cunning or resilience.

Would time-traveling clinical psychologists diagnose a bipolar disorder from the Atondo record? They might well. Here are telltale signs: Atondo's periodically unsettled, erratic behavior, insomnia, inflated self-esteem, and sudden urges and appetites suggest manic episodes. There are his false starts at monastic life; his desertion from the army; his secret flirtation while serving in the Franciscan convent in Orizaba followed by his sudden departure from the convent without so much as a word to the friars or the woman he was courting; the obsession with fashionable clothing; the hasty marriage in Mexico City and equally hasty abandonment of his young wife and child; more unplanned departures and arrivals; the logorrhea and tall tales mentioned by witnesses, especially the inflated claims of courage and loyalty to the crown in his encounters with insurgents. And then there are the long, tearful episodes of guilt and regret that followed, usually accompanied by illness, possibly psychosomatic.

Using modern medical terminology to explain Atondo's *picaro*-like behavior risks confusion as well as clarification, but his fit across the range of medical opinion and debate about bipolar disorders is strong. While specialists warn against seeing manic depression in every case of erratic behavior,[22] and bipolar disorder is still a moving target for clinicians, three kinds of bipolar disorders are widely recognized: bipolar I, a late-onset, less severe form of both mania and depression that appears not to run in families; bipolar II, a "milder" form of the illness than bipolar III, with prolonged "hypomanic" episodes of disinhibited, euphoric behavior followed by periods of depression; and bipolar III, or borderline personality disorder, a severe, persistent manic-depressive disorder that may render the person helpless and lead to institutionalization.[23]

The poet and mental-health advocate Bassey Ikpi describes her bipolar II diagnosis this way:

This brain constantly in conference with the racing heart, reminding me to slow down, stay calm. . . . So damn excited to be alive at that moment. You could do anything. Now imagine feeling that every day for a week, or a month, or a few months. Twenty-four hours a day, seven days a week, without a break. The first week or so, it's great. Until it's not. . . . And you *have* to write the entire book tonight before you can sleep or eat or leave the house or do anything. But first you *have* to call your friends and your sister and the guy you just met and tell them all how much you love them. Tell each one that you've never felt this way about any other human being in the entire world and you're so lucky and so glad and so grateful to have such an amazing, magical person in your life. And you believe it because it's true. Until it isn't. Until everything about them . . . starts to make you feel like your blood is filled with snakes. . . . You want to bury your hatred in them, but you're never quite sure who you hate the most. You, it's always you. . . . Because if you can't sleep because you can't stop thinking of the perfect jeans or the shirts so soft they made Oprah moan, then you can just buy them and try them for yourself. And imagine you do all of this each night for many nights. . . . Imagine you don't fit anywhere, not even in your own head.²⁴

Like many people who live with this kind of bipolar disorder, Atondo's full-blown symptoms were intermittent. He was never judged insane and placed in one of the urban asylums, nor was he considered bewitched and subjected to exorcisms.²⁵ Unsteadily, erratically, this young man made his way along the margins of society for close to fifteen years—until he openly impersonated a priest and began to say Mass and hear confessions.

Atondo in 1815 would not have understood himself as acutely ill and ultimately not responsible for his actions; nor would the Inquisitors who judged him, although mania and depression had been described and sometimes linked as medical conditions since the time of the Greek physician Aretaeus in the first century CE.[26] Although the Inquisitors took the unusual step of keeping him out of circulation in the Inquisition prison for three years without final judgment, they did not raise the possibility that Atondo suffered from some kind of madness. Perhaps it was because his symptoms did not seem to have rendered him helpless. But there was another, compelling reason: if he were judged mad, he could not be held responsible for his actions. In that case, he would have been eligible for absolution and possible release or placement in an asylum. Instead, his episodes of euphoria and depression, betrayals, tall tales, and imposture were taken to be the moral failings of a damaged soul. Atondo did not disagree, but he sensed that something was physically wrong, even if he had no words to express it except a well-worn metaphor. As he told the tribunal, he suffered from a "great debility of the heart" ("suma debilidad de su corazón").

Conclusion

Did Aguayo and Atondo see themselves as kin to the literary *pícaros*? Did officials and acquaintances consider them *pícaros*? Whether or not they knew of Guzmán de Alfarache, Lazarillo, and other characters from literature, their lives and actions do fit some of the most familiar traits. As young men, they were unsettled, self-absorbed social orphans from poor families, making their way by lying, cheating, and stealing if need be. They were not to be trusted. Both drew on their education and familiarity with the sacramental duties of priests to successfully impersonate them for a time. Both spoke of their ancestors as Old Christians, and they may have aspired to a life of leisure and authority, but they lived too close to the edge of destitution to be idle for long. The written record is silent about whether either was spontaneously witty and habitually insolent—as Diego de Torres Villarroel, the aforementioned author and mathematics professor who was a self-styled *pícaro* in his youth, thought a proper *pícaro* should be—although surely insolence and wit were less in character for Atondo, and both were too preoccupied with themselves to be knowing rebels against society's inequalities and injustices.

Atondo's tidal mood swings, which suggest an underlying bipolar disorder, better explain his erratic, sometimes outrageous behavior than does a *pícaro*'s crafty manipulation of a wicked world. He was a vulnerable, sad figure, intermittently self-destructive and overwhelmed with guilt. He suffered and did not hesitate to pour out his inner turmoil in writing, where he lied badly, contradicted himself repeatedly, said too much, and was inclined to exaggerate. In the end, he was not like any of the hearty survivors among the literary *pícaros* he might have read or heard about.

Aguayo sometimes acted like a literary *pícaro*, whether he styled himself as one or not. But he was different in that he was more picaresque than any of them, except Quevedo's Pablos. Writing about Guzmán de Alfarache, José Antonio Maravall spoke of the "radical solitude of the *pícaro*,"[27] but Aguayo was less attached to others than were any of the fictional *pícaros*. And, rather than a bald-faced liar like Pablos, Aguayo was a specialist in half-truths, protean in the strategic ways he would reveal himself only partly, even under the duress of incarceration and threat of torture. Unlike the literary *pícaros*, he seemed to have taken a page from Gracián (or perhaps

Dale Carnegie, avant la lettre) on winning momentary friends and influencing people. In spite of his protestations of remorse and contrition, and in spite of the Inquisitors' ministrations to his immortal soul, he was a rogue to the end. He also endured as much punishment as any of the literary *pícaros*: four hundred lashes plus lengthy exile, confinement, and penal servitude.

When Aguayo and Atondo acted in picaresque ways that a reader of the classic novels would have recognized, did they model themselves on those literary characters? Or was the influence at least as much in the other direction, as the trickster stories based on local life in northern New Mexico suggest? Did Alemán and Fernández de Lizardi build their characters and moral messages from people and conditions they knew or observed, more than they inspired the behavior of young rascals? Gauging the literary imagination and sociological acumen of authors of picaresque novels and their direct influence is beyond my reach. Even the influence of one author on another is elusive. Fernández de Lizardi wrote about *pícaros* and found them in everyday Mexican life, but he did not mention Alemán or his novel in print, much less any other picaresque novel. However, Fernández de Lizardi's contemporary, the public intellectual and bibliographer Father José Mariano Beristáin de Souza, noticed the similarities between *Periquillo Sarniento* and *Guzmán de Alfarache*. Likewise, Aguayo and Atondo make no literary references—nothing like Bernal Díaz del Castillo's mention of the popular romance of chivalry, *Amadís de Gaula*, to convey the astonishment he felt at his first glimpse of Aztec Tenochtitlan in 1519—to suggest that they were somehow inspired to act as they did because they knew about literary *pícaros* and their doings. But the possibility of life drawing from literature cannot be dismissed. Whether or not Aguayo and Atondo read picaresque novels, what matters is that they shared something of the picaresque frame of mind and behaved in ways recognizably picaresque as the standard dictionary of the time construed the term. But there is also a tantalizing lapidary phrase in one of Aguayo's confessions that echoes more directly the sentiments of Guzmán de Alfarache, Lazarillo, and Pablos going off on their own as wide-eyed, incautious juveniles in a hostile world. Quevedo's Pablos declares himself "consoled by the thought that I would have to make my way by my own abilities."[28] For his part, Aguayo wrote that he left home as a teenager "with a mind to seek my life . . . for good or for ill."[29] And even Atondo seemed to echo a fellow sower of discord from literature, Guzmán de Alfarache, in his late-blooming, self-fashioned pursuit of Christian righteousness, striving to do good in a threatened, sinful world. Like Guzmán, Atondo presented himself in his last recorded words as a sort of human watchtower, peering into the heart of things, sounding a warning and taking action.

By the eighteenth century, the *pícaro* in literature and local life had become a stock character of Hispanic popular culture, little more than a scoundrel for many.[30] But the word was packed with more meaning than a given speaker or writer may have intended, with something for almost everyone, including Aguayo and Atondo—deplorable, dangerous, subversive, and impudent, or comical, largely harmless, even admirable when *pícaros* exposed the pretensions and deceptions of others and moved toward (or, for some admirers, resisted moving toward) personal redemption in conventional Catholic terms.

Conclusion

"The quarry is an actual and therefore not fully knowable individual moving within the actual and therefore not fully penetrable world."

—INGA CLENDINNEN[1]

Aguayo and Atondo were not fictional characters, not cardboard mountebanks or buffoons, not literary symbols of rebellion and social dissolution. Nor were they just object lessons of redemption squandered and souls lost, as the Inquisitors would have it, or cheeky idlers who survived solely by their wits or begging.

Beyond Pícaros

There is more to their humanity than labels like *pícaro* and bipolar suggest, although *pícaro* and bipolar at least invite more complex and dynamic understandings than "phony," "heretic," "rebel," "charlatan," and "hypocrite." And there is much about their lives that remains obscure or approachable only in the subject's version of his past as he recalled it under duress. Atondo's taste for fashionable clothes comes through in his testimony, but there is no physical description of him or his outfits. For Aguayo's years in Cuba, there is little more than his sketchy account, sprinkled with obvious omissions and likely half-truths, and there is room to wonder whether he was the utter loner he claimed to be. Furthermore, the inquisitorial setting for the investigations and trials, and the fact that the Inquisition collected and arranged most of the evidence, meant that important matters were left untouched or were framed in particular ways. For instance, the tribunal took little interest in their crimes against persons, even when they were impersonating priests; and if either man favored religious tolerance, the chambers of the Inquisition were not where he was likely to say so.[2] Nevertheless, the written record we have for them is a blessing when it comes to the historian's search for the metaphors our subjects lived by.[3] To Atondo, it came down to the heart, that perplexing seat of his physical and spiritual being that had led him astray, but also led him, he assured the Inquisitors, to the urgent certainty that many souls were in jeopardy in this time of godless politics, and he needed to act. Aguayo was less inclined to speak metaphorically for the record, but the *pícaro* in several of its contemporary meanings and literary incarnations—skillful at deception, unapologetically shameless, witty and fluent, a nimble rogue—seems to have been his guiding metaphor. He saw himself as a poor but clever underdog going it alone in a heartless world.

The similarities between these two impostors dim further by considering other differences that also show Atondo as less picaresque and Aguayo more so. To begin with, they stand at opposite ends of Erving Goffman's scale of how performers understand themselves in their roles in his classic *The Presentation of Self in Everyday Life* (1956). At one extreme is the performer who is completely taken in by his own performance, as Atondo was when he went on his confessing spree in the vicinity of Aculco. At the other extreme is the instrumental performer who observes and calculates. Like Aguayo, he is not taken in by his own act.⁴ Atondo earnestly prepared to *be* a confessor; Aguayo prepared to play the role. These poles of Goffman's scale are not necessarily fixed, but it was only Atondo who moved back and forth across the line between being and pretending to be, sincerity and pretense.

Aguayo was a master of face-to-face deception, but he was also a self-styled *hombre a secas*. He never married or mentioned lovers, and claimed to have no friends. He shared the loner's part with the confidence man, who emerged as something of a North American culture hero in the mid-nineteenth century: the socially marginal swindler-manipulator awakening mixed feelings of admiration, amusement, and disgust.⁵ Like Early Modern *pícaros*, the con man appeared in a time of rapid, unstable change and displacement that had loosened the fit between appearances and social position. But the con man, whether a character like P. T. Barnum or Herman Melville's "confidence man," felt no twinge of conscience, no regret for the mischief and harm he did. The same could be said of Aguayo, but in one essential respect he was not a classic con man. He remained largely an outsider in his social order, focused on surviving the present, while the confidence man looks to the future and "gradually aligns himself with social power and takes . . . over."⁶ Aguayo operated on the *pícaro*'s smaller stage, in hit-and-run deceptions. He offered no greater reason for his actions than self-preservation, but, in his evasive way, he was more daring and defiant than Atondo. Apparently for him, the thrill of living on the edge and the pleasure of duping others while basking briefly in their regard were more compelling than the likelihood of being found out and punished. More calculating and deliberate than

Atondo in his crimes against people, Aguayo was also quicker to exit when he saw trouble coming.

Both men repeatedly took flight, but for different reasons. Aguayo was moved by an impulse to personal freedom, to escape confinement or avoid arrest. Atondo was less predictable. His departures usually were flights from responsibility to others or from messes of his own making, and were soon followed by dependence on yet another person or institution. Not by nature a freedom-seeking loner, much of the time he was compliant, anxious to please superiors, whoever they might be. Unlike the literary *pícaro* who is constantly going forward into one new experience after another, he backtracked and alternated, with three Franciscan periods, two tailoring ones, two military ones, and two insurgency ones. Temporarily he had romantic attachments, including at least two dalliances and a brief marriage. But he was awkward and nervous in speech, inclined to say too much and exaggerate, and unable to trade effectively in clever lies. His turbulent and painful inner life spurts forth in tall tales, verbose accounts of his actions and feelings, angst-ridden introspection, and befuddlement. Not surprisingly, Aguayo, the usually self-contained, circumspect wordsmith, was more adept at currying favor, which he understood to be less about pleasing than persuading as he crossed Baltasar Gracián's line from dissimulation to simulation.

The contrast in their religious lives and displays of emotion is especially striking. Atondo's fitful religious "inclination" bordered on a mystical sense that he had been chosen by God to defend the Church. For Aguayo, the Catholic liturgy and doctrine were part of a practice he had grown up with and found to be useful cultural knowledge, whatever his beliefs may have been. Atondo was a bundle of nerves, needing to show and tell others how he felt. His writings were cries for help, as well as appeals for mercy and not-very-successful attempts to fathom his own sudden urges. In his written confession, Atondo was candid, confused, and less than completely truthful, all at once. Long on self-pity and self-regard, he recognized that he didn't know his own heart, but was certain it governed his actions. Aguayo rarely expressed his feelings to the tribunal or eyewitnesses. Self-pity and soul-searching were not his way. He let slip during his first trial an angry comment about being rejected by his father, made a routine show of remorse to the Inquisition before sentencing, and lamented the loss of his youth after returning from Cuba. That was about it. He had no intention of offering the Inquisition a complete narrative of his life.

Aguayo and Atondo were by no means the only impostors at large in early Latin America, and they cast short shadows compared to characters like Catalina de Erauso (discussed in the introduction) or Gregor MacGregor, with his outsize ego, grandiose plans, and hunger for acclaim. MacGregor served in the British army without distinction in his youth until he left for South America in 1810 to join anti-Spanish insurgents in Venezuela and Central America. Again he did not distinguish himself, but when he returned to Britain in 1821 he presented himself as the Cazique (lord) of Poyais, a putative paradise of fertile lands and temperate climate facing the Caribbean in Central America, awaiting colonists and investors. The land sale and settlement scheme benefited no one but MacGregor, and him not much. He eventually moved back to Venezuela, claimed to be a hero of the liberation, and brazened his way to citizenship and the honorary rank of general. But little is known of MacGregor and his ways, or of most other impostors of the time, beyond the swindles and a juicy personal story or two.[7] For the most part, their lives and thoughts pass unrecorded.

Enric Marco, an impostor of our time, is better known, inside and out, and provides an opportunity for closer comparison between Aguayo and Atondo. Marco reinvented himself as a celebrated figure in Spain after the death of Francisco Franco in 1975. A restive but inconspicuous young opportunist and grifter in the 1930s and 1940s, he abandoned two wives and several children and kept a low profile politically during the Franco years. In middle age Marco had the urge and summoned the nerve to persuade others that he had been an intrepid anarchist officer during the Spanish Civil War, escaped to France in 1939, returned to Barcelona as a resistance fighter against the Franco government, was captured and sent to a Nazi concentration camp near the German border with Czechoslovakia in 1941, and later was imprisoned by the Franco regime for political activity. None of this was true. As a teenager he *had* favored the Republicans in Barcelona and served as a corporal, and he *had* gone to Germany in 1941, but as a volunteer worker in Nazi war factories, looking to avoid compulsory military service in Franco's army. He *had* been imprisoned briefly in Spain during the Franco years, but as a common criminal. Heralded by the late 1970s as a war hero, Holocaust survivor, and resolute warrior against fascism, Marco wrote articles, gave interviews, made scores of stirring speeches at Holocaust and Civil War commemorations, received awards, briefly served as general secretary of the revived CNT (the former confederation of anarcho-syndicalist trade unions), and for many years was president of Spain's largest association of Holocaust survivors.

What made Marco tick? Remarkable research by Benito Bermejo and a probing study by Spanish novelist Javier Cercas have some answers. Marco's gift for this kind of impersonation depended on his ability to tell his gripping stories with conviction and verve. Even in his eighties and nineties, he remained energetic, charming, flirtatious, and witty, an experienced performer who had been telling self-serving lies since childhood. For much of his life he seemed to be an ordinary man, a face in the crowd who did the predictable thing, saying whatever best served his interests and appealed to the audience of the moment, unusual mainly in his energetic, outgoing manner and high need to be admired. But in the 1970s he was able to capitalize on this keen sense of what people wanted to hear, recognizing that Spaniards were eager to lift up a common man of the left who had survived the nightmares of the Civil War and the Holocaust. Cercas calls him a loner who refused to be alone, whose compulsive need for approval and admiration was driven by an inflated sense of himself as "a great man, generous, loyal, and profoundly humane, a tireless fighter for good causes, and this was why so many people said wonderful things about him."[8] Evidently Marco more than half believed his own fantastic stories of heroic deeds and tribulations even while purposely altering the record books of the Flossenbürg concentration camp to make it seem that he had been interned there.[9] Despite protestations of regret when particular lies were exposed, he continued to lie whenever the proof against him was not conclusive. Cercas concludes that he repented nothing.

Do Aguayo and Atondo resemble Marco? All three were restless survivors, self-centered schemers, and opportunists from an early age, lacking much empathy for others. All three were literate and had some talent for performance—a great talent in Marco's case. None of them had strong family ties growing up, or abiding friendships as adults. Of the three, Aguayo was the resolute loner and most self-sufficient, if not an introvert, but all of them had the interpersonal skills to make their way in society and work their scams for a time. They appealed to popular values—such as piety, truth, and repentance for Atondo and Aguayo; bravery and social justice for Marco—even as their actions undercut them.

There are other three-way resemblances, but comparing Marco to Aguayo and Atondo separately sharpens the differences between the two colonial Mexican impostors as well as the singularity of Marco. Aguayo shared with Marco the habit of building plausible lies out of half-truths. Both were unrepentant. Both were adept performers, always acting, sizing up the audience. But unlike Marco, Aguayo the solitary escape artist did not mistake the performer for the performance. He knew he was not who he pretended to be. The closer one looks, the more both of them remain mysteries, like peeling an onion to reveal another layer rather than the crux of a categorical answer.

The resemblance between Marco and Atondo runs deeper. Both were inordinately eager to please and be respected, likely to utter whatever flattery they thought suited the moment. Unchecked by periods of lethargy and depression, Marco proved especially skillful at this, even when his effusive compliments were transparently excessive and insincere. Like Marco, Atondo avoided being alone. He sought out masters and patrons, though his behavior was too erratic to keep them. In Cercas's judgment, Marco was a full-fledged narcissist, with the classic inflated sense of his own importance, needy for attention and admiration, and indifferent to the feelings and interests of others. During his manic periods, Atondo was a match for Marco in this way, too, regarding himself as a hero and martyr. Like Marco, he was not just playacting. But as performers, neither Atondo nor Aguayo could hold a candle to Marco the appalling narcissist—the needy, gregarious, dynamic liar who ran toward the spotlight when his golden opportunity arrived, stumbling into his story of suffering and heroism, then covering his tracks ingeniously and succeeding magnificently for years.[10]

But talent, cunning, and wit alone do not account for successful impersonations. There can be no such characters without tolerant institutions and a receptive audience ready to be taken in, believing in some larger promise, and all three impostors were alert to what their audience wanted. We may goggle at their shameless audacity and guile, but they owed much of their success to the collective failure of the people they deceived and a prevailing culture of equivocation and deception. As the celebrated Peruvian writer and politician Mario Vargas Llosa put it, Marco "exploited our incurable penchant for fiction."[11] Like Aguayo and Atondo, he appealed to convictions and sentiments held dear at the time, to a taste for simple truths and a desire for someone like the person he seemed to be. Some would argue that civil society itself depends on a faith that most communication can be trusted most of the time, as if we are wired to trust.[12] But is this "default to truth" timeless and uniform across cultures and within a given society? I don't think so. In the case of Early Modern Spain and Spanish America, where the default was at least as much toward suspicion and *engaño* as presumption of truth, the circumstances for successful deception and presumption of truth were more specific. Here the figure of the priest was widely respected, his services were both required and coveted, and he was identifiable by the way he dressed and how he carried himself.

There was no shortage of ordained priests at the time, but few were willing to take up their calling in poor and remote settlements. As impersonators of priests, Aguayo and Atondo often headed for the villages and towns that did not have a full-time priest. People there may not have heard Mass in months and were more likely to welcome them and what they offered, especially the blessings of the sacraments, even if the appearance and behavior of this visiting priest did not seem quite right. For the most part, people in Mexican cities during the eighteenth century also looked to priests to sanctify their lives and destinies, but impostors had less room to slip in unobtrusively because ordained clergymen alert to bogus interlopers were concentrated there. As hit-and-run priests in rural areas, Aguayo and Atondo could be gone before suspicion led to arrest. They found trouble when they offered their services in larger towns, although even there, Aguayo succeeded in deceiving the *padre guardián* of Toluca and the accountant at León.

Fugitive Freedom

It is tempting to write about people and events as if free will or accident reigns, or economic considerations, misery, or the social milieu determine. If choice has a place in the life stories of Aguayo and Atondo, what kind of freedom did they seek and find? *Libertad* was a watchword of the time, invoked by many kinds of people in different situations, but what did it mean to them?[13] To twenty-first-century readers, the meaning of liberty most associated with the eighteenth century has to do with the European Enlightenment's questioning spirit and pursuit of freedom for the individual to act as he (and sometimes she) pleased, short of violating the commandments of God, at least for Spanish liberals and Mexican insurgents who tried to reconcile religion and Jean-Jacques Rousseau. In this sense, *libertad* meant individual rights and free will as a near-absolute good, a celebration of the autonomous inner self freed from the arbitrary constraints of society and its institutions. In public life, in practice, there would have to be a balance between personal freedom and the rights of everyone, but the inalienable rights now would include equality before the law and personal freedoms, as well as religious toleration and a questing, questioning spirit meant to free critical reason from the shackles of religious dogma. Behind this capacious view of liberty was the idea of personal improvement, even perfectibility—that individuals are born innocent, not inevitably corrupted by original sin.[14]

An older, still prevailing notion of *libertad* regarded personal freedom with suspicion—as an invitation to irresponsibility, licentiousness, and irreverence. Ordinary citizens, in particular, could not be trusted with too much freedom. Without the order imposed by society and institutions of the state, they were like "Moors without a lord" or "feral cattle." Liberty needed to be kept in check or the result would be social and political chaos. This traditional notion of individual liberty subordinated to the interests of the community and the state was warmly embraced in the eighteenth century by Bourbon reformers who regarded themselves as men of the Enlightenment, but muffled the philosophes' invitation to equality before the law and personal freedoms. Their interest in the unfettered mind centered on "useful knowledge"—mainly science and engineering applied to agriculture, mining, medicine, urban planning, and construction—and social reforms intended to bring greater order and prosperity to society at large and more power and stability to the government. The neoclassical architecture and arts that stood for Bourbon order, grandeur, and modernity echoed the Roman Empire more than the Roman Republic. Progress in this pale Enlightenment was about order, obedience, practicality, productivity, and improvement, not a revolution of the mind.

Aguayo, Atondo, and the Inquisitors were largely outside the currents of political and intellectual change that reshaped the meaning of liberty, the high politics of Spain and Spanish America in the 1810s, and the reinvention of government in Mexico thereafter. If they were rebels, they were rebels without a cause. Aguayo and Atondo tried to dodge the Bourbon reformers' old and new institutions of order, rather than oppose them head-on. If Aguayo, testifying forty years earlier, was partial to the philosophes' freedom of conscience and personal liberties, he didn't let on. Atondo was aware that political changes were in the wind, but declared himself a champion of the good old order ordained by God and king. Writing in early 1816, after the Spanish constitution of 1812 and its partisans had challenged the monarchy and temporarily failed, Atondo declared, "I lived by the written laws of the Holy Fathers, not by those of today being imposed by reckless men who have given themselves over to depravity."[15]

Aguayo's and Atondo's freedom was closer to that of the early literary *pícaros* than to that of French philosophes and revolutionaries—leaving home, traveling light, and making their way by brash deception and outright lies. Aguayo's thirst for status, like that of Guzmán de Alfarache, Pablos, or the young Periquillo, brought him close to an idea about personal freedom, but he understood it selfishly as a capacity to have his way at the expense of others. What kind of freedom is there in being on the run, moving away from rather than toward something, looking over one's shoulder for the judicial police or adversaries and former victims, preparing for the next deception, keeping one's story straight? Aguayo and Atondo got away with their frauds for a time by being on the move in this large, complex society of late colonial central Mexico that combined hierarchy with spatial mobility, inviting fraud when it depended on external markers of status rather than a well-earned local reputation for competence and honesty. Aguayo and Atondo broke out of confinement, but not into the radical Enlightenment's promised land of free will. They were free to take a chance on lying and stealing, but if this was freedom, it was an anxious, lonely kind, warped by self-absorption and betrayal. Especially after impersonating priests and corrupting the sacrament of confession, they were in too deep to turn back. Theirs was a fugitive freedom in the double sense of *fleeing* and *fleeting*: dodging or breaking out of confinement; and evanescent and unsettled, slipping away. The wonder is that they survived as long as they did.

Enric Marco was talented and cunning, but his remarkable success and more settled, celebrated life of deceit depended on fortunate timing and a receptive audience. In the heady years after Franco's death, many Spaniards were sprucing up their personal histories, preparing to reclaim some part of Spain's past as a workers' republic. They were ready to welcome just such a hero as Marco seemed to be. Atondo also had his chance to play the hero during Mexico's decade-long struggle for independence, when self-conscious Mexicans were feeling their way toward new political identities. But while Marco kept a low profile during and immediately after Spain's Civil War, Atondo was too well known to the Inquisitors and civil authorities during the War of Mexican Independence to slip through the cracks and reinvent himself later. He had neither covered himself in glory as an insurgent nor succeeded in convincing royalist authorities in power that he had steadfastly championed their cause and lectured insurgents on the evil of their ways, as he claimed. (If he was the avid royalist he claimed to be, it is odd that he did not volunteer his services to the crown or that royalist leaders did not reach out to him as a prize recruit.) If he had lived into the 1820s, it is a good bet that he would not have risen to fame and glory in a Marco-style grand deceit. He was too unsteady, his stories too far-fetched, and the public trail of his bunglings and betrayals too long.

Might Aguayo have enjoyed something like Marco's public acclaim if he had been a young adult during or after the independence struggle? As with all counterfactual possibilities, it is impossible to know, but lucky timing has a way of drawing out hidden abilities in individuals who would otherwise remain inconspicuous. After all, there was little in José María Morelos's life as a less-than-model pastor in a backwater parish of the lowlands of Michoacán in the early 1800s to predict that he would become one of the most gifted military and political leaders during the early years of Mexico's independence wars, and immortalized as a great national hero after 1821.

But Morelos and Marco had something in common that Aguayo and Atondo lacked: a social network that connected them politically to leaders and a base of support at just the right time. Marco was friendly with activist university students who became his enthusiastic promoters after Franco's death. Morelos had met Miguel Hidalgo at the Colegio de San Nicolás in Valladolid during his student days and was welcomed into Hidalgo's loose-knit independence movement when he inquired about its purposes a month after Hidalgo issued his manifesto for independence in September 1810.[16] Atondo's erratic behavior wrecked his family ties and affiliations with Franciscans in Orizaba, Querétaro, and Mexico City—connections that might have proved useful on either side of the independence struggle. Aguayo's only apparent network consisted of a few fellow prisoners, and his disastrous alliance with one of them put him off network-building later. Given the opportunity in the 1810s, he might have become a mercenary insurgent, mouthing the new ideology of freedom and equality. The resentment was there, and he was from Guanajuato, in the heart of the Bajío region, where the insurgency began. But judging by his deep suspicion of organizations and personal loyalties he probably would have abstained; and, like Atondo, he was too well known as a small-time villain who had impersonated priests. His career as a durable super-*pícaro* might have made him a legend among other outcasts, but not a revolutionary hero.[17]

. . .

"I decided to go to the Indies to see if by changing my world and surroundings my luck would improve. But things went worse as they always do when one only changes the scenery and not old habits and a way of life."

—FRANCISCO DE QUEVEDO, *La vida del buscón*[18]

Aguayo and Atondo were remarkable survivors, and at last report they were still alive, giving their written histories a glimmer of picaresque hope. But it was almost certainly too late for another curtain call or redemption. The written record probably ends because they, too, were very close to the end. At forty-two in 1792, Aguayo was old by the standard of the time, and his body had taken a beating. The Inquisition evidently was content to let him molder in the squalid Guanajuato municipal jail that he knew well and had long tried to avoid. At thirty-two in 1816, Atondo was younger, but not young, and in poor health and worse spirits. His Inquisition dossier ends without a verdict, either because he died in the cells or because the judges and staff were too occupied with the precarious situation of their tribunal to complete the trial, in which case he might have been released after those three years in prison, sick and defenseless, without prospects or family.

Neither Aguayo nor Atondo was the threat to civic order and spiritual salvation that colonial authorities seemed to think they were, but both were a source of confusion, and reckless reverence in one case and irreverence in the other, in their treatment of the sacraments and impersonation of priests. Subversion may not have been their aim, but their unruly kind of freedom could not be ignored. Aguayo never gave up his *pícaro*'s fugitive freedom, limited as it was. On the run from himself and his missteps most of his life, Atondo hardly experienced freedom at all. The closest he came to sensing what freedom for some higher purpose might be came to him with pen in hand in the dismal cells of the Inquisition. There he imagined himself a martyr to his Catholic faith, confronting godless insurgents in Mexico's independence wars: "I saw the Catholic Faith so forsaken that I was moved to do what I have done. And if by my example this situation is remedied, I willingly resign myself to suffer whatever consequences may please God and Your Most Illustrious Sir."[19] Was Atondo trying to please his audience again, as he had tried many times before? No doubt, but, sick and dejected after his years in the Inquisition jail, he probably believed what he said. In any event, there is nothing to suggest that either Atondo or Aguayo had bitten the apple of the Rights of Man or embraced the paradox of freedom in community. For them, there was no possibility of a bourgeois happy ending such as José Joaquín Fernández de Lizardi granted his reformed *pícaro*: "Since that cruel winter, everything has been springtime, with your mother, I, and yourselves living together and enjoying peace and innocent pleasures in our modest but honorable circumstances, which, while not furnishing me with the means for superfluous luxuries, has given me everything I need, so that I have never envied the fate of rich men and potentates."[20]

Notes

Introduction

1. R.H. Tawney, *The Agrarian Problem in the Sixteenth Century* (New York: Longmans, Green, 1912), 268.

2. Hugh Thomas, *Conquest: Montezuma, Cortés, and the Fall of Old Mexico* (New York: Simon and Schuster, 1993); Hugh Thomas, *Rivers of Gold: The Rise of the Spanish Empire* (London: Weidenfeld and Nicolson, 2003); Hugh Thomas, *The Golden Empire: Spain, Charles V, and the Creation of America* (New York: Random House, 2010); Hugh Thomas, *World without End: Philip II and the First Global Empire* (New York: Random House, 2015).

3. "A la espada y el compás, más y más y más y más." Epigraph from Bernardo de Vargas Machuca, *Milicia y descripción de las Indias* (Madrid: Pedro Madrigal, 1599).

4. Sean F. McEnroe, *A Troubled Marriage: Indigenous Elites of the Colonial Americas* (Albuquerque: University of New Mexico Press, 2020), xxvii.

5. As Brian Owensby writes, "The relative peace of colonial New Spain resulted not from the generalized application of force or from simple domination. It sprang from the very success Indian communities had in carving out a space for themselves, a space they ardently defended and amplified through litigation." Brian Owensby, *Empire of Law and Indian Justice in Colonial Mexico* (Stanford, CA: Stanford University Press, 2008), 308. The great structural changes that swept across Europe and the New World from the sixteenth century on are not easily summarized, and several approaches to description and explanation have been advanced. One that largely ignores Latin America and

Spain but gives ideology its due is Thomas Piketty, *Capital and Ideology* (Cambridge, MA: Harvard University Press, 2020). See especially Piketty's discussion in chapters 1, 2, and 7 of changes in power and property relationships during the Early Modern Period—halting, uneven shifts from a society of orders, in which the clergy and nobility predominated in just about every way, toward "ownership societies," in which modern, centralized states, private property, and market forces came to hold sway. For Spain, and especially New Spain, while a centralizing state developed, the ongoing power of the Church as a propertied institution and the clergy as leading educators, intellectuals, and spiritual, moral, and social leaders prevailed until well into the nineteenth century, along with coercive labor institutions and the enduring presence of hereditary, albeit domesticated, nobles and public aspirations to nobility.

6. See the discussion in William B. Taylor, *Theater of a Thousand Wonders: A History of Miraculous Images and Shrines in New Spain* (New York: Cambridge University Press, 2016), 36–38.

7. One of the few studies of sixteenth-century colonization in New Spain that give pride of place to widespread disorder, shadow institutions, and disobedience is Martin Nesvig's book about Michoacán, *Promiscuous Power: An Unorthodox History of New Spain* (Austin: University of Texas Press, 2018). See also his "Religious Chicanery in Michoacán's Emergent Church," *Colonial Latin American Review* 17, no. 2 (December 2008): 213–32. However, there is abundant scholarship going back fifty years or so that complicates a story of a Spanish-made, more or less crystallized colonial system. One of the fruitful recent areas of research in this direction is legal history, questioning "law's capacity to 'tame' the unordered circumstances of cultural difference." Brian P. Owensby and Richard J. Ross, eds., "Introduction," in *Justice in a New World: Negotiating Legal Intelligibility in British, Iberian, and Indigenous America* (New York: New York University Press, 2018), 1. For a close look at how distance shaped the documents that served as instruments of administration in the early Spanish empire see Sylvia Sellers-García, *Distance and Documents at the Spanish Empire's Periphery* (Stanford, CA: Stanford University Press, 2013).

8. For a vivid sense of the unsettled lives and feelings of returning veterans see chapter 5 ("Home from War") in Miguel Martínez, *Front Lines: Soldiers' Writing in the Early Modern Hispanic World* (Philadelphia: University of Pennsylvania, 2016).

9. Bartolomé Bennassar, *Recherches sur les grandes épidémies dans le nord de l'Espagne à la fin du XVIe siècle. Problèmes de documentation et de méthode* (Paris: SEVPEN, 1969); Vicente Pérez Moreda, "The Plague in Castile at the End of the Sixteenth Century and Its Consequences," in *The Castilian Crisis of the Seventeenth Century*, ed. I.A.A. Thompson and Bartolomé Yun Casalilla (Cambridge, UK: Cambridge University Press, 1994), 32–59; Jaime Vicens Vives, *An Economic History of Spain*, trans. Frances M. López-Morillas (Princeton, NJ: Princeton University Press, 1969), 348–50.

10. Official fears about vagabondage appear in various royal edicts and ordinances. One example was quoted in the 1737 edition of the *Diccionario de la lengua castellana . . .,* compiled by the Real Academia Española: that they "bring great harm to our kingdoms" ("grande daño viene a los nuestros reinos"). Another word that signified "vagabond" in seventeenth- and eighteenth-century Spain, *mostrenco*, implied that wanderers were less than human. According to Sebastián de Cobarruvias's 1610 *Tesoro de la lengua castellana o española*, *mostrenco* meant a stray, untamed animal as well a placeless, masterless vagrant with no apparent means of support. Madness and witchcraft—both of which made for other kinds of strangers—became especially prominent social issues for the governing classes and a wider public in Europe at this time, although the beginnings of physicians treating madness as a psychological condition would come later, in the eighteenth century. See Roy Porter, *Madness: A Brief History* (Oxford: Oxford University Press, 2002), 127–32. On madness in the Early Modern Period see also Michael MacDonald, *Mystical Bedlam: Madness, Anxiety, and Healing in Seventeenth-Century England* (Cambridge, UK: Cambridge University Press, 1981); H.C. Erik Midelfort, *Mad Princes of Renaissance Germany* (Charlottesville: University Press of Virginia, 1994); H.C. Erik Midelfort, *A History of Madness in Sixteenth-Century Germany* (Stanford, CA: Stanford University Press, 1999). For Spain, there is the ingenious blending of Inquisition records and Golden Age fiction by Dale Shuger, *Don Quixote in the Archives: Madness and Literature in Early Modern Spain* (Edinburgh: Edinburgh University Press, 2012). With dire consequences, witch crazes sporadically gripped much of Christian Europe, whether Catholic or Protestant, during this period from the mid-sixteenth century to the early eighteenth century. Women were the usual targets. The literature on witch hunts in Early Modern Europe is vast. Two convenient places to begin are Brian Levack, ed., *The Oxford*

Handbook of Witchcraft in Early Modern Europe and Colonial America (New York: Oxford University Press, 2013); and LuAnn Homza, "Witch Hunting in Spain: The Sixteenth and Seventeenth Centuries," in *The Routledge History of Witchcraft*, ed. Johannes Dillinger (London: Routledge, 2020), 134–44.

11. María Jiménez Salas, *Historia de la asistencia social en España en la Edad Moderna* (Madrid: Consejo Superior de Investigaciones Científicas, 1958), 39–40. There may have been many more. Dale Shuger cites a contemporary source estimating five hundred thousand beggars and paupers by 1608, and perhaps one million by 1617. Dale Shuger, *Don Quixote in the Archives: Madness and Literature in Early Modern Spain* (Edinburgh: Edinburgh University Press, 2012), 17.

12. Jiménez Salas, *Historia de la asistencia social en España en la Edad Moderna*, 39, 43.

13. Javier Herrero made this point to explain how the first picaresque novel, *La vida de Lazarillo de Tormes y de sus fortunas y adversidades*, sprang from an intellectual milieu in Spain in the 1540s in which legislation and theological disputes on poverty and vagrancy had risen to the top of public discourse. Javier Herrero, "Renaissance Poverty and *Lazarillo*'s Family: The Birth of the Picaresque Genre," *PMLA* 94, no. 5 (October 1979): 876–86.

14. Paul Slack, *The English Poor Law, 1531–1782* (New York: Cambridge University Press, 1995); Paul Slack, *From Reformation to Improvement: Public Welfare in Early Modern England* (Oxford: Oxford University Press, 1999); Sidney Webb, *English Poor Law History*, 3 vols. (London: Longmans, 1927–63). Poor relief and policing in the Italian states, which were generally more charitable, have also been well researched. Among Nicholas Terpstra's works, see *Cultures of Charity: Women, Politics, and the Reform of Poor Relief in Renaissance Italy* (Cambridge, MA: Harvard University Press, 2013), especially the introduction and chapter 2.

15. Jiménez Salas, *Historia de la asistencia social en España en la Edad Moderna*, 38.

16. Linda Martz, *Poverty and Welfare in Hapsburg Spain: The Example of Toledo* (Cambridge, UK: Cambridge University Press, 1983), 5, 32, 91, 123, 159; and Jiménez Salas, *Historia de la asistencia social en España en la Edad Moderna*, viii and chapter 4, emphasize that the response to paupers in Spain beginning in the sixteenth century stressed greater charity and charitable institutions.

17. Norman F. Martin, *Los vagabundos en la Nueva España: Siglo XVI* (Mexico: Edit. Jus, 1957), 63, 75.

18. At first glance, it would seem that Spain conceived of citizenship at home and in the colonies in a remarkably liberal way that welcomed full membership for outsiders: that if one acted like a citizen, through residence, membership in the Catholic Church, and integration into the community, which included fealty to the Spanish monarchy, one could be regarded as a citizen. But integration and citizenship depended crucially on whether the community regarded the aspirants as truly Catholic and loyal, permanent members of the community, with a recognized place there. If not, they "could be rejected as foreigners," writes Tamar Herzog in *Defining Nations: Immigrants and Citizens in Early Modern Spain and Spanish America* (New Haven, CT: Yale University Press, 2003), 140. Whether in Spain or in the colonies, people who were doubted could be excluded or treated as lesser members of the community. Herzog's book is devoted to the subtleties of this inclusion and denial of citizenship among Spaniards and foreign Europeans in Spain and Spanish America during the Early Modern Period. Into the eighteenth century, some displaced, impoverished Christian Spaniards were desperate enough to find a place and gain membership in a community to present themselves as Muslim strangers seeking Christian baptism in a particular parish and accepting adoption by, or service to, their new godfather and his family in the bargain. Thomas Glesener, "Se (re)faire musulman. L'accès des pauvres intinérants aux droits de la conversion (Espagne, XVIIIe siècle)," *Revue d'histoire moderne et contemporaine* 64, no. 2 (April–June 2017): 129–56.

19. "Limpiar la república de vagamundos y de gente de mal vivir . . . pues semejante gente sólo sirve de corromper las costumbres, introducir vicios y cometer crímenes." Norman F. Martin, "Pobres, mendigos, y vagabundos en la Nueva España, 1702–1766: Antecedentes y soluciones presentados," *Estudios de Historia Novohispana* 8 (1985): 122.

20. New Spain's beggars and rootless poor still await their historian. In addition to Norman F. Martin's *Los vagabundos en la Nueva España*, there is his article "Pobres, mendigos y vagabundos en la Nueva España, 1702–1766: Antecedentes y soluciones presentados," *Estudios de Historia Novohispana* 8 (1985): 99–126.

21. Martz, *Poverty and Welfare in Hapsburg Spain*, esp. 4, 236, attributes the migrations to cycles of natural disaster. Anne J. Cruz, *Discourses of Poverty: Social Reform and the Picaresque Novel in Early Modern Spain* (Toronto:

University of Toronto Press, 1999), 21; and José Antonio Maravall, *La literatura picaresca desde la historia social (siglos XVI y XVII)* (Madrid: Taurus, 1986), 10, point to early capitalist enterprises contributing to social and economic crises and impoverishment in the sixteenth and seventeenth centuries, but without elaborating.

22. Jiménez Salas, *Historia de la asistencia social en España en la Edad Moderna*, 39–40.

23. "Entraban desnudos y en el mismo año salen vestidos con oro y plata para gasto de dos años." Jiménez Salas, *Historia de la asistencia social en España en la Edad Moderna*, 39–40.

24. Fernando Díaz Plaja, *The Spaniard and the Seven Deadly Sins*, trans. John Inderwick Palmer (New York: Charles Scribner's Sons, 1967): "A very marked social scale provides each Spaniard with an inferior on whom he impresses his own authority and to whom he stands as chief. . . . When we reach the beggar it looks as if we have come to the bottom. To whom can this man display his primacy? For one, to the same person from whom he receives the alms. . . . In receiving alms the poor Spaniard does a favor in his turn: he is putting the giver on the road to salvation, to heaven" (14). For the original see Fernando Díaz Plaja, *El español y los siete pecados capitales*, 25th ed. (Madrid: Alianza Editorial, 1992): "Una marcadísima escala social provee a cada uno de los españoles con un inferior, al que hacer sentir la propia autoridad y ante el que sentirse jefe. . . . Al llegar al mendigo parece que hemos dado en el fondo. ¿Ante quién puede ése manifestar su primacía? En primer lugar, ante el mismo de quien recibe la limosna. . . . Al aceptar la limosna, el pobre hace a su vez un favor: pone al donante en el camino de la salvación, del cielo" (24–25). Cruz acknowledges this ethos, but suggests that it was largely a thing of the past by the seventeenth century. Cruz, *Discourses of Poverty*, 96.

25. "Buen nombre y fama y lo que prometen las Indias." Andrés de León (Fr. Martín de León y Cárdenas), *Historia del Huérfano*, ed. Belinda Palacios (Madrid: Fundación José Antonio de Castro, 2017), 23.

26. An *hidalgo* is defined in the 1780 edition of the *Diccionario de la lengua castellana* as a "noble person from a known ancestral home and land, exempt from the taxes paid by commoners" ("la persona noble que viene de casa y solar conocido, y como tal está exento de los pechos y derechos que pagan los villanos").

27. John Lynch, *Spain under the Habsburgs* (Oxford: Blackwell, 1964), 1:263. Henry Kamen provides a more literal translation: "I would prefer to lose all my dominions and a hundred lives if I had them, because I do not wish to be lord over heretics." Henry Kamen, "Toleration and Dissent in Sixteenth-Century Spain: The Alternative Tradition," *Sixteenth Century Journal* 19, no. 1 (Spring 1988): 19.

28. For a contrast to Philip II's dogmatic view and a spirit of intolerance in the sixteenth century see Kamen, "Toleration and Dissent in Sixteenth-Century Spain," 3–23; Stuart B. Schwartz, *All Can Be Saved: Religious Tolerance and Salvation in the Iberian Atlantic World* (New Haven, CT: Yale University Press, 2008). The latter finds currents of religious tolerance even in the Early Modern Period.

29. Miriam Eliav-Feldon, *Renaissance Impostors and Proofs of Identity* (New York: Palgrave Macmillan, 2012) explores the idea that in Early Modern Europe (for her, mainly the 1480s to the 1630s) many people assumed false identities, or at least were suspected of imposture. She focuses mainly on persecution of new Christians, witches, mystics, and gypsies as suspected impostors.

30. For this distinction and attributing simulation to commoners see Michael Gordian, "The Culture of Dis/simulation in Sixteenth- and Seventeenth-Century Europe" (PhD thesis, Warburg Institute, University of London, 2014).

31. In his study of defensive dissimulation—of religious minorities in Early Modern Europe dissembling in order to protect themselves—Perez Zagorin treats simulation and dissimulation as virtual synonyms, but then makes the distinction that was fundamental to Spanish commentators of the time: "In a strict sense dissimulation is pretending not to be what one actually is, where simulation is pretending to be what one actually is not." Perez Zagorin, *Ways of Lying: Dissimulation, Persecution and Conformity in Early Modern Europe* (Cambridge, MA: Harvard University Press, 1990), 3.

32. An English translation, *The Art of Worldly Wisdom*, has been in print since 1924 and was something of a best seller in the 1940s and the 1960s. Both Zagorin and Valentin Groebner recognize Gracián's place in promoting the art of dissimulation in Early Modern Europe. Zagorin, *Ways of Lying*, 8; Valentin Groebner, *Who Are You? Identification, Deception, and Surveillance in Early Modern Europe*, trans. Mark Kyburz and John Peck (New York: Zone, 2007), 217.

33. *Exceder*—to go too far—is one of his favorite words of warning.

34. "El amigo es más necesario que el fuego y el agua, hay tan pocos que provean de ella." León, *Historia del Huérfano*, 43.

35. By way of comparison, Diego de Ocaña, the multitalented Hieronymite alms collector who carried devotion to Spain's Nuestra Señora de Guadalupe to South America and left behind fascinating writings and artworks, has been the subject of remarkable recent studies that convey much about his private and public self, as well as about Spanish America at the turn of the seventeenth century. See especially the following articles by Kenneth Mills: "Mission and Narrative in the Early Modern Spanish World: Diego de Ocaña's Desert in Passing," in *Faithful Narratives: Historian's Religion, and the Challenge of Objectivity*, ed. Andrea Sterk and Nina Caputo (Ithaca, NY: Cornell University Press, 2014), 115–31; "Ocaña's Mondragón in the 'Eighth Wonder of the World,'" in *Texts and Voices from Colonial and Postcolonial Worlds*, ed. Arun W. Jones (College Park, PA: Penn State University Press, forthcoming); "Una sacra aventura en tierras que se volvían santas: Diego de Ocaña, O.S.H., 1599–1608," *Allpanchis* (forthcoming).

36. Based on a manuscript in Sevilla's Archivo General de Indias, the "autobiography" may have been composed in the mid-1620s, when Erauso presented herself at court with a printed *relación de méritos y servicios* (formal enumeration of services rendered to the king) requesting recognition of her heroic deeds on behalf of the crown in the Americas.

37. A similar case at the end of the eighteenth century of an outspoken Spanish woman who passed as a virile man in South America and secured papal permission to dress in men's clothing is discussed in Thomas A. Abercrombie, *Passing to América: Antonio (Née María) Ytá's Transgressive, Transatlantic Life in the Twilight of the Spanish Empire* (University Park, PA: Penn State University Press, 2018). Abercrombie concludes that María Ytá's identity as Antonio Ytá was understood by the subject, and nominally accepted at the time, as an act of self-transformation rather than a deception. For a male example of manly courage on the battlefield that also merited pardon from the crown and pope for serious crimes in the early seventeenth century see León, *Historia del Huérfano*.

38. An example of a manly woman as folk hero in late colonial Mexico is María Sánchez, an early eighteenth-century ranch owner and celebrated horse trainer in the Valley of Oaxaca. A story in the 1777 *relación topográfica* for San

Martín Tilcajete tells of a neighboring rancher wagering that María could not wrestle one of his wild colts to the ground with her bare hands. She proceeded to prove him wrong and won the colt in the wager. By 1777, the pointed hill near her ranch was called "la teta de María Sánchez," as it is today. Biblioteca Nacional, Madrid, Mss #2449-50.

39. There has not been a systematic study of impersonators of priests and *comisarios*, but Nesvig notes five cases for sixteenth-century Michoacán (1555, 1565, 1576, 1581, and 1599) in "Religious Chicanery," 213-32; Javier Villa-Flores notes three cases for Chiapas in the 1640s and two for Hidalgo in 1645 and 1666 in "Wandering Swindlers: Imposture, Style, and the Inquisition's Pedagogy of Fear in Colonial Mexico," *Colonial Latin American Review* 17, no. 2 (December 2008): 251-72; Ilarione da Bergamo mentioned seeing two in the *auto de fe* of 1768, as noted in Robert Ryall Miller and William J. Orr, eds., *Daily Life in Colonial Mexico: The Journey of Friar Ilarione da Bergamo*, trans. William J. Orr (Norman: University of Oklahoma Press, 2000), 151; John F. Chuchiak notes that two of the thirteen individuals presented in the 1783 *auto de fe* in Mexico City were priest impersonators in *The Inquisition in New Spain, 1536-1820: A Documentary History* (Baltimore: Johns Hopkins University Press, 2012), 177-81; and Matthew O'Hara writes that "dozens of individuals were brought before the Inquisition for posing as clerics," without citing dates and places, in "The Orthodox Underworld of Colonial Mexico," *Colonial Latin American Review* 17, no. 2 (December 2008): 233-50. O'Hara's main subject in this article is several groups of laymen in late colonial Mexico City and the city of Querétaro pretending to be friars. The Inquisition treated them more leniently than the priest impersonators, likely because they had not administered sacraments to unsuspecting confessees.

40. Sylvia Sellers-García's deeply researched essay "Walking while Indian, Walking while Black: Modern Policing in a Colonial City" (forthcoming in *American Historical Review*) explores poignant aspects of crime and the move toward greater law-and-order policing in late eighteenth-century Guatemala City.

41. The staff disputes were less among members of the three-judge panel than between senior administrators, who as a rule were peninsular Spaniards, and their junior colleagues, the creole *familiares*. Richard E. Greenleaf, "The Inquisition Brotherhood: Cofradía de San Pedro Mártir of Colonial Mexico," *The Americas* 40, no. 2 (October 1983): 171-207.

42. See for example Bruno Feitler, "The Inquisition in the New World," in *The Cambridge History of Religions in Latin America*, ed. Virginia Garrard-Burnett, Paul Freston, and Stephen C. Dove (New York: Cambridge University Press, 2016), 133–42. Greenleaf notes, "Perhaps it was a sense of frustration in coping with the larger problems that led the Holy Office to concentrate on smaller ones. The tendency to engage in hairsplitting and tedious controversies over jurisdiction and judicial competencies was one result of this frustration." Richard E. Greenleaf, "The Mexican Inquisition and the Enlightenment, 1763–1805," *New Mexico Historical Review* 41, no. 3 (July 1966): 190–91. Although they do not focus on changes in the operations of courts of the Inquisition or the eighteenth century in particular, the essays in Charles H. Parker and Gretchen Starr-LeBeau, eds., *Judging Faith, Punishing Sin: Inquisitions and Consistories in the Early Modern World* (Cambridge, UK: Cambridge University Press, 2017), offer an ambitious, wide-ranging approach to Early Modern religious discipline that includes both Catholic and Calvinist ecclesiastical courts.

43. Monelisa Lina Pérez Marchand, *Dos etapas ideológicas del siglo XVIII en México a través de los papeles de la Inquisición* (Mexico: El Colegio de México, 1945).

44. See especially Richard E. Greenleaf, "The Inquisition in Spanish Louisiana, 1762–1800," *New Mexico Historical Review* 50, no. 1 (January 1975): 45–72. It would be a mistake to generalize far from the Louisiana case. Inquisition agents evidently did not spend much time looking for seditious ideas where they were not to be found. Greenleaf's study of the activity of Inquisition *comisarios* in another frontier province, New Mexico, during the eighteenth century noted that they concentrated on perennial moral misbehavior that violated the Ten Commandments, proper devotion, and the authority of the Church: bigamy, adultery, deviant sex, blasphemy, and witchcraft. The Inquisition did not have jurisdiction over Pueblo Indians, so the investigations by *comisarios* in New Mexico concerned the Spanish and *casta* populations. No doubt the focus would have been on sorcery in Pueblo communities if that had been within the tribunal's purview. Richard E. Greenleaf, "The Inquisition in Eighteenth-Century New Mexico," *New Mexico Historical Review* 60, no. 1 (January 1985): 29–60.

45. Between forty and fifty individuals tried by the Mexican Inquisition during the colonial period were handed over to crown officials for execution.

Those who repented at the stake were thought to free their souls from eternal damnation.

46. Italian Capuchin friar Ilarione da Bergamo, who traveled in New Spain in the 1760s, witnessed the *auto de fe* of March 1768 and remarked that "the throng of people was beyond number." Miller and Orr, *Daily Life in Colonial Mexico*, 152.

47. For punishments before 1700: floggings in 14.3 percent of cases, exile in 13.8 percent, public shaming in 6.8 percent, reclusion in a convent in 6.3 percent, galley service in 5.7 percent, and fines in 5.3 percent. Chuchiak, *The Inquisition in New Spain*, 50.

48. Richard Boyer, *Lives of the Bigamists: Marriage, Family, and Community in Colonial Mexico* (Albuquerque: University of New Mexico Press, 1995), appendix, 233ff. Nora E. Jaffary found 102 cases of feigned mystics, more than half of them processed during the eighteenth century, with a concentration from 1775 to 1801. Nora E. Jaffary, *False Mystics: Deviant Orthodoxy in Colonial Mexico* (Lincoln: University of Nebraska Press, 2004), cases listed in appendix 1, 177–87. For Spain, Andrew W. Keitt found a spike in cases of false mystics and other kinds of feigned sanctity before the Inquisition during the second quarter of the seventeenth century. Andrew W. Keitt, *Inventing the Sacred: Imposture, Inquisition, and the Boundaries of the Supernatural in Golden Age Spain* (Leiden, the Netherlands, and Boston: Brill, 2005), 91.

Chapter One

1. AGN Inquisición 1376 exp. 6, fols. 21–22, 1769–70 (which skirts the question of his racial designation); AGN Inquisición 1172 exp. 12, fols. 367ff, 1771; AGN Inquisición 1096 exp. 9, 1773, fol. 170r. All subsequent quotes regarding Aguayo come from these sources.

2. Prison sentences were rare. Aguayo was held in prison on various occasions for months at a time awaiting trial and judgment.

3. "Con el ánimo de buscar mi vida . . . por vien o por mal."

4. Aguayo was released at his father's request, which suggests that the father had been behind the arrest, perhaps charging his son with theft. "Having been imprisoned in my homeland at my father's request. When I was released I went to him as his son": "haviendo sido prisionero en mi patria a

petición de mi padre de la que salí y fui puesto a su preciencia como hijo de familia." AGN Inquisición 1376 exp. 6, fols. 133–36.

5. "Me arrimé a la sombra de una pobreza"; "bolví a mi dicho padre para ber si me deje con alguna ropa."

6. His father comes into the record only once more, during the second trial in 1773, when he presents Aguayo's baptismal record.

7. "En donde mi propia pobresa me obligó."

8. "Porque los carceleros de dicha viya me desnudaron de una capa y otros trapos por echarme de la prición."

9. "Habriendo el misal en las partes donde él lo abrió."

10. The length of a league varied some, since it amounted to the local ground an able-bodied person or pack animal ordinarily could cover in an hour. For the maps in this book, a league is taken to be about three miles.

11. The record of Antonio de Ribera's short Inquisition trial in Mexico City in December 1770 and January 1771 on suspicion of having freed Aguayo is in AGN Inquisición 1172 exp. 12, fols. 360–93. Ribera initially denied helping Aguayo escape, and said several times that he declined Aguayo's entreaties. The Inquisition concluded that Ribera had abetted Aguayo's escape by not impeding him, but had not directly assisted him. Ribera was allowed to return to Texmelucan after paying seven pesos and one half-*real* to cover the costs of his incarceration, a sum equal to the proceeds of the shirt and *relicarios* he had received from Aguayo and sold.

12. "Pero él, con gran sagacidad engañó al Notario diciéndole que fuera con él a la parte en que avía dexado sus papeles: y luego que no tenía títulos ni licencias porque estaba cuatro meses ha suspensó a causa de una herida que dió a un soldado. Con esto, y no sé qué amenaza, amedrentó al imperito Notario y desapareció de este valle. Hoy he tenido noticia que dixo missa en la Magdalena, que es dos leguas de aquí, un pueblito de sólo indios que no sabrán practicar el negocio."

13. "Indio chico de cuerpo, flaco, pálido, y aspecto como de diez y siete a diez y ocho años."

14. "Tengo causas graves en este Sto Tribunal, quiero de una bes reconsiliarme y confesar mis delictos."

15. "Herege apóstata de nuestra santa fe cathólica o a lo menos sospechoso de serlo, despreciados de los santos sacramentos."

16. "Si el rigor del derecho huviéramos de seguir lo pudiéramos condenar en grandes y graves penas, mas queriéndolas moderar con equidad y misericordia por algunas causas justas respecto que a ello nos mueben."

17. The Aguayo-Solano affair in the Guanajuato jail and the corridors and cells of the Inquisition is documented in AGN Inquisición 1096 exp. 9 and 1078 exp. 13.

18. "Having heard of the great power of this Holy Tribunal to free him from the sentence and punishment corresponding to his escape": "haver oido decir el mucho poder que tenía este Santo Tribunal para libertarle de la pena y castigo que le correspondía de la fuga."

19. "Pero que en la realidad de verdad era falso y mentir . . . para proporcionar mejor los medios de que se le trajese a este tribunal."

20. "Pe, estoi en el n. 16. ¿Qué has dicho?"

21. "Lo hizo puramente con la boca, no de corazón."

22. "Reo de hereje apóstata vehementemente sospechoso de falsario notoriamente"; "incompatible con una fe firme y constante de la doctrina de la Yglesia."

23. "Apelo con la devida humildad, recignación y toda veneración como devía."

24. "Experimentando los maiores rigores de la más dura prisión, oprimido con todo género de tormentos que la más cauta prudencia puede conciderar."

25. Francisco de Quevedo, *Lazarillo de Tormes and The Grifter: Two Novels of the Low Life in Golden Age Spain*, trans. David Frye (Indianapolis: Hackett, 2015), 96. "Adonde ya no tenía qué sacar más de mi sombra." Francisco de Quevedo, *La vida del buscón*, ed. Fernando Cabo Aseguinolaza (Barcelona: Crítica, 1993), 105.

26. "Hayarme tan sonrrojado y confuso"; "mis muchos y enormes delictos . . . los herrores y maldades que mi pequeñes ha cometido . . . [y la] gravedad tan grande que eran mis herrores."

27. In this first trial, Aguayo bluntly blamed his father: "Bad upbringing at the hands of my father has been the main cause of my downfall": "culpando el mal gobierno de mi Padre que ha zido la maior causa de mi perdición."

28. "Mal Christiano abusado de las dogmas de la Fe."

29. "Bien sabe Dios las lágrimas que he derramado de Dolores culpas acá en mi soledad"; "pido con toda mi alma, obediente a recibir . . . la penitencia que este Santo Tribunal me imponga en su mucha caridad."

30. "La devida humildad, recignación y toda veneración como devida es a la notoria venignidad que piadosa obstenta este Santo Tribunal"; "los berdaderos penitentes que piden misericordia con todo mi corazón."

31. "Suffering all sorts of torments that the most searching intelligence can hardly imagine": "experimentando los mayores rigores de la más dura prisión, oprimido con todo género de tormentos que la más cauta prudencia puede conciderar."

32. "Hablaba quedito y de forma que los concurrentes no entendiesen su ignorancia."

33. "Habriendo el misal en las partes donde él lo abrió."

34. "He has not had reliable or friendly company, and has only been with those individuals he chanced to meet on the road": "que no ha tenido compañía segura ni amistosa y que sólo se ha acompañado de aquellos sugetos que por casualidad hacían el mismo camino."

35. The files mainly show him in contact with fellow inmates during his incarceration in the early years, in one case noting a simple social hierarchy among them. He saw some of the same inmates in different jails, exchanging information and gossip with them.

36. "Reo fugitivo y reincidente."

37. "Olvidado de las obligaciones y profesión Christiana con grabe daño y ruina de su alma . . . pospuesto el Sto temor de Dios y abandonando el respeto y veneración a la rectitud y justicia de este Santo Tribunal y de las santas determinaciones de la Yglesia, pasándose de su puro y santo gremio al feo impuro y abominable de los hereges lutheranos. . . . Despreciados de los santos sacramentos y jurisdicción de las llabes de la Yglesia perjuro y escandaloso acostumbrado a cometer otros muchos más oy menos graves delitos del fuero y conocimiento de este Sto Oficio."

38. In the early 1550s, Pope Julius III had pointedly recommended mercy in cases of heresy.

39. Luis R. Corteguera explores the case and offers this interpretation in *Death by Effigy: A Case from the Mexican Inquisition* (Philadelphia: University of Pennsylvania Press, 2012).

40. "O te digo verdades o mentiras." Quoted in Carroll B. Johnson, "Defining the Picaresque: Authority and the Subject in *Guzmán de Alfarache*," in *The Picaresque: Tradition and Displacement*, ed. Giancarlo Maiorino (Minneapolis: University of Minnesota Press, 1996), 177.

41. On life expectancies at this time and place see Robert McCaa, "The Peopling of Mexico from Origins to Revolution," in *A Population History of North America*, ed. Michael R. Haines and Richard H. Steckel (Cambridge, UK, and New York: Cambridge University Press, 2000), 275.

42. On this sense of being above manual labor see Américo Castro, *The Spaniards: An Introduction to Their History*, trans. Willard F. King and Selma Margaretten (Berkeley: University of California Press, 1971), 610.

43. "Yndito en traxe de clérigo"; "movido de compación"; "con mucho gusto por exercitarse en un acto tan heróico de charidad qual es la veneración . . . a los señores sacerdotes especialmente pobres que assí procuró obsequiarlo quanto pudieron sus cortedades."

44. "Espuestos mis pobres y miserables carnes a una pública vergüenza, de suerte que estoy en el día constituyendo un berdadero símbolo de compación y miseria capás de merecer el blando."

Chapter Two

1. The only important manuscript source I have located for Atondo is Bancroft Library, University of California, Berkeley Mss 96-95m, vol. 23. There is also a short record in AGN Inquisición 1421 exp. 24, fols. 184-86, which amounts to the missing cover pages for the Bancroft Library manuscript. It is called "Relación de la causa seguida en este Santo Oficio contra Fr. Juan Atondo Sánchez, religioso laico de la Regular Observancia, de estado casado, por confesante y celebrante sin órdenes."

2. "All my relatives treat me as enemies and had me sent to the Acordada prison": "convocáronse todos mis parientes en enemigos míos y me pusieron en la Acordada."

3. "Mi corazón encendido en el amor de Dios y la Religión." This would have been either in the Dieguino convent at the west end of the Alameda near the center of Mexico City (which housed the Pinacoteca Virreinal until 2000), or in the convent at Churubusco (where the Battle of Churubusco was centered in 1847). According to H. H. Bancroft, there were a total of fourteen Dieguino convents in Mexico before they were disbanded. H. H. Bancroft, *History of Mexico* (San Francisco: A. L. Bancroft, 1883-88), 6:591.

4. The missionary college at Orizaba was founded in 1799. Thirty-five friars were in residence in 1826. Francisco Morales, "Mexican Society and the

Franciscan Order in a Period of Transition, 1749–1859," *The Americas* 54, no. 3 (January 1998): 347.

5. "Mi obstinado corazón."

6. He went on to say that he received in return a gold crucifix and many food treats (*bocaditos*).

7. In this case he was arrested by the Acordada, an elite armed police force and criminal court organized on military lines, created in 1722.

8. Morales, "Mexican Society and the Franciscan Order in a Period of Transition," 347. There were ninety friars in residence there in 1786 (324). The number of *donados* is not given by Morales, but there must have been a dozen or more to serve a community of this size.

9. "Que más acepto a los ojos de Dios era tomar un fusil para los enemigos de la Patria."

10. "Que los Mandamientos de la Leyes de Dios los rezaba al derecho no al revés como allí se haría." In one of his asides, Atondo went on about a sermon by a Carmelite friar he heard at the insurgent encampment.

11. "Que con tanta desvergüenza y poco respeto respondía a un Señor Coronel, le dije que para mi no era coronel sino mi hermano, que lo conozía por la marca que tiene de ser hijo de mi Padre San Francisco."

12. "Visto que no podía seducirme . . . dio cuenta que yo era . . . mui nocivo y seduciría a los soldados a que dejara aquel partido tan injusto."

13. "Visto la necesidad que ai por fuerza de un sacerdote forastero."

14. A Bula de la Santa Cruzada was a Papal bull granting indulgences (remissions of the punishment of sins) to those who made donations in support of the crusades against Muslims, pagans, and heretics.

15. For the sake of secrecy, in this case where many priests served as witnesses and reporters at a politically fraught time, the Inquisition did not record the names of informants.

16. John F. Chuchiak, *The Inquisition in New Spain, 1536–1820: A Documentary History* (Baltimore: Johns Hopkins University Press, 2012), 129–31.

17. "Ardiente amor . . . ardiente deseo"; "con exasperado ahinco"; "llorando amargamente"; "no hallando otro más eficaz remedio que llorar y arrepentirme de mis pecados"; "no era por malicia sino un efecto de su atolondramiento y congoja que experimentaba en este sacrílego acto"; "lo digo con lágrimas en los ojos y con los pulsos temblando."

18. "Con todo corazón"; "corazón afligido"; "me oprimía el corazón"; "obstinado corazón"; "que tranquilizara su corazón"; "los intentos de mi corazón."

19. "Mis enormes delitos"; "gran pecador"; "mi depravada malicia e iniquidades"; "mis maldades"; "hize muchas trácalas"; "mi mala vida"; "tan escandalosos y criminales excesos"; "mi apetito torpe"; "hasta aquí he vivido como . . . un demonio"; "convertí en un demonio"; "soy el más malo de quantos tiene el mundo."

20. "Pido perdón"; "verdadera penitencia."

21. "Imploro su misericordia"; "no hallando otro eficaz remedio que llorar y arrepentirme de mis pecados."

22. "Convertí en demonio"; "de humilde en soberbio."

23. He wrote several times of his own grief in the same breath as the grief of Christ's Passion ("hallándome en tan grande congoja"; "la congoja de la Pasión"), and his description of his body covered with sores "like a leper" may have brought to mind the suffering of Job.

24. Instances of seeing himself as a demon include "convertí en demonio, de humilde en soverbio" (I changed into a demon, from humble to arrogant) (over clothes at Orizaba); his crimes during the alms mission as either "sugestión del demonio o ignorancia" (at the suggestion of the devil, or ignorance); and his statement that he had lived like a *demonio* to this point.

25. "Ven amigo y te daré lo que tu tanto trabajas por llevarte un alma"; "pero la Soberana Reyna y Madre de Pecadores no lo permitió, que si no lo hago según mi exasperación y lejos de tirarlo lo vesé y me dio temor"; "comenzó Dios, como buen Padre, a darme inspiraciones y yo negando la obediencia."

26. "Me llené de ánimo y confianza de que sería perdonado de todos mi pecados (fue para mi concepto hize una buena confesión)." He said he proceeded to tell the truth "according to the sentiments of his conscience": "según los sentimientos de su conciencia."

27. The lay witness who contradicted Atondo was an *española* who said she declined to confess to Atondo when he invited her and her family to do so because she had a regular confessor and suspected that Atondo was not a priest.

28. Vega's guide went through many editions—at least seventeen published in Spain from 1656 to 1812, plus four in Catalan, and translations into Dutch, French, Portuguese, and Italian. I read the 1812 edition published in

Madrid by Viuda de Barco. Vega's professed aim was to elicit full confessions with true contrition that would lead to personal reform and salvation.

29. "Así porque le escridriñaba su conciencia con arreglo a los Mandamientos de Dios y de la Yglesia, como por sus exortaciones con que procuraba encenderlo en la verdadera caridad."

30. "Por medio de mis consejos se remediaban aquellas almas que havían perdido el camino verdadero."

31. "Me determiné a confesarlo, y diciendo lo siguiente me senté en la sacristía, se arrodilló."

32. "Un estudiante se havía condenado por callar pecados en la confesión, haviendo callado uno de deshonestidad, hizo mucha penitencia; su maestro lo amaba mucho por sus virtudes y tenido por justo entre todos su compañeros; caió enfermo de la enfermedad de la muerte, y le administraron los Santos Sacramentos y con lágrimas supuestas que parecían de contrición, murió y se condenó: su Maestro que deseaba saber qué suerte le havía cabido, oró por él y estando en oración se le apareció dando fuertes gemidos y diciendo no ores por mi, que estoi condenado; respondió el Maestro, cómo ha sido eso con tanta penitencia que hacías; respondió y dijo: es verdad que la hazía, pero callé un pecado en la confesión por vergüenza y me he condenado para que veas lo que padezco."

33. "Tras muchas cosas y comenzó su confesión, y reconosido mi miseria y la contrición de dicho penitente, me confundí y reconocí; . . . e . . . hízele ver otras cosas muchas de la Pasión de JesuCristo y Dolores de María Santísima, con lo que derramó muchas y copiosas lágrimas por lo que me persuadí a ser bueno lo que yo hazía en el deseo hermano."

34. "Vi tan perdida la Fee Católica que esto me movió hazer lo que he hecho."

35. His precise words: "No ai pena que baste para ser castigado."

36. "Esto me movió hazer lo que he hecho y si con hazer un exemplar con mi persona se remedia, pronto estoi y resignado a sufrir todo quanto sea de agrado de Dios y de V.S. Yllma"; "me pareze haver sido por caridad y por otra parte puede haver sido soverbia y amor propio."

37. "Quando cometí mis delitos ignoraba que era caso de Ynquisición, aunque no ignoraba que era mal porque sabiendo que era pecado no debía haverlo cometido."

38. "A pocos días nos fuimos para Puebla, . . . y llegando hallá me puse a recapazitar y entrar dentro de mi, iendo una noche más por curiosidad que por

devoción entré a los exercicios que se hazen en la Compañía de Jesús y oiendo una plática acerca de lo que en mi pasaba que me pareció por mi lo decían, intiman[do] el Padre la Misericordia de Dios y lo mucho que havía padecido por librarnos de las penas eternas y que por muchos que fueran los pecados, mucho más era su misericordia y que con una gota de sangre de la que derramó por nostoros en la Cruz era bastante para nuestro remedio. . . . Con esto me llené de ánimo y de confianza de que sería perdonado de todos mis pecados."

39. "Haviendo conocido por los sentimientos de su corazón."

40. "Suma debilidad de su corazón; los violentos impulsos de su corrompido corazón."

41. "Que no obstante asegurar los confesados por este reo parecía buen confesor por los consejos y exemplos . . . se deduce haverse portado con sobrada indiscreción e imprudencia y que causaría graves daños en el mismo sacramento. . . . No sólo confesó en salud a muchos, sino que a más de haver publicar lo havía hecho con uno que iban a fusilar, absolviéndole de las excomuniones."

42. "Sobrada indiscreción e imprudencia . . . causaría graves daños en el mismo sacramento de la salud"; "ningún respeto a la religión que profesa."

43. "Cárzeles secretas de este Santo Oficio se ha sostenido en llamarse religioso, dejar abrir cerquillo y corona y firmar sus declaraciones con el título de Fray Juan Atondo, infiriendo la maior injuria a este Tribunal y despreciando su autoridad como si no fuera capaz de descubrir . . . sus engaños, averiguando con toda exactitud no haver sido Atondo más que un triste donado que no profesó."

44. "Se persuadió ser bueno lo que hazía, pues creiendo el penitente que era sacerdote y teniendo contrición, juzgó sería perdonado por la palabra que Jesuchristo enseñó en la doctrina que el que tuviere contrición, aunque haia cometido los maiores pecados del mundo, al punto se le perdonan y pone en gracia de Dios."

45. "Una ilusión diabólica"; "una refinada hipocresía para engañar."

46. His hypocrisies included the instructions he gave to penitents in the confessional. Did he himself ever make a full confession? Also, wearing the blue habit of the Franciscan Order in public represented the priest's suppression of his personal appetites and desires, and his commitment to obey God's will. Atondo admitted that he had done neither.

47. "No por la Potestad que yo tenía que era ninguna, pero por la palabra que Jesuchristo por la doctrina nos enseña en el deseo hermano que por la

contrición aquel que la tuviere aunque haia cometido los maiores pecados." Atondo seemed to see himself acting on the same obligation that moved the whiskey priest in Graham Greene's *The Power and the Glory* (1940).

48. Rudolf Otto, *The Idea of the Holy*, trans. John W. Harvey, 2nd ed. (Oxford and New York: Oxford University Press, 1958).

49. "Ser un hombre de dos lenguas y que sólo trata de adular al mundo y convenir con todos"; "fueron tantas sus palabras y tantos sus discursos inconexos y aun contradictorios que al punto conoció que era hombre de mala fe."

Chapter Three

1. First published in serial form in 1816, Fernández de Lizardi's novel *El Periquillo Sarniento* has remained in print ever since.

2. From James Tate, "A vagabond" (2013), in *Selected Poems* (Middletown, CT: Wesleyan University Press, 2013), 232, copyright James Tate, used by permission.

3. Joseph Campbell, *The Hero with a Thousand Faces* (Princeton, NJ: Princeton University Press, 1949), 18.

4. Howard Mancing, "The Protean Picaresque," in *The Picaresque: Tradition and Displacement*, ed. Giancarlo Maiorin (Minneapolis: University of Minnesota Press, 1996), 274.

5. On the female possibility see chapter 7, "The *Pícara*: The Rogue Female," in Peter N. Dunn, *The Spanish Picaresque Novel* (Boston: Twayne, 1979), 113-33.

6. Mancing suggests a "canon" of twenty-five to thirty titles in "The Protean Picaresque," 282-86. Peter N. Dunn finds that only in the loosest sense can about twenty Spanish works of the sixteenth and seventeenth centuries be regarded as picaresque. Peter N. Dunn, *Spanish Picaresque Fiction: A New Literary History* (Ithaca, NY: Cornell University Press, 1993), 5. In a narrow sense, Mateo Alemán's *Guzmán de Alfarache* (Madrid: Cátedra, 1984) is the one novel of the period that fits the genre as most literary historians conceive it.

7. Claudio Guillén, "Toward a Definition of the Picaresque," in *Literature as a System: Essays toward the Theory of Literary History* (Princeton, NJ: Princeton University Press, 1971), 72, 74, 98. The scholarship tends to separate into lumpers—model builders focused on genre genealogy—and splitters, who say the models blur fundamental differences and historical links among individual works (Peter Dunn, for one; Michel Cavillac, for another).

8. "No se ha de querer ni aborrecer para siempre. Confiar de los amigos hoy, como enemigos mañana, y los peores. . . . Con los enemigos, siempre puerta abierta a la reconciliación." Baltasar Gracián, *Obras completas*, ed. Miguel Batllori and Ceferino Peralta (Madrid: Atlas, 1969), 1:422.

9. Anne J. Cruz, *Discourses of Poverty: Social Reform and the Picaresque Novel in Early Modern Spain* (Toronto: University of Toronto Press, 1999); José Antonio Maravall, *La literatura picaresca desde la historia social (siglos XVI y XVII)* (Madrid: Taurus, 1986). Maravall recognizes that poverty and vagrancy were not unique to Spain, but thinks they were much worse there—"con mucha mayor gravedad" (762).

10. Anonymous, *Lazarillo de Tormes and The Grifter: Two Novels of the Low Life in Golden Age Spain*, trans. David Frye (Indianapolis: Hackett, 2015), 6, 7. "Procura de ser bueno, y Dios te guíe"; "en aquel instante desperté de la simpleza en que como niño dormido estaba . . . pues solo soy." Anonymous, *La vida de Lazarillo de Tormes*, ed. H. J. Chaytor (Manchester: Manchester University Press, 1922), 4, 5.

11. Anonymous, *Lazarillo de Tormes and The Grifter*, 51. "Pues, en este tiempo estaba en mi prosperidad y en la cumbre de toda buena fortuna." Anonymous, *La vida de Lazarillo de Tormes*, 48.

12. The expurgated version—the *Lazarillo castigado*—has only recently received close attention as a text in its own right. See Felipe Ruan, "Literary History, Censorship, and *Lazarillo de Tormes castigado*," *Hispanic Research Journal* 17, no. 4 (2016): 269–87; and especially Reyes Coll Tellechea, *Lazarillo castigado: Historia de un olvido muerte y resurrección de Lázaro* (1559, 1573, 1884; repr., Madrid: Ediciones del Orto; Minneapolis: University of Minnesota Press, 2010). Coll Tellechea notes that the expurgated version eliminated two chapters and phrases and sentences elsewhere, not all of which had been criticized by priests. The net effect of the changes was to make Lázaro the cause more than the victim of his misfortunes and depraved moral state.

13. Guillén insists that these two novels sustained the emerging genre, "not singly but conjointly." Claudio Guillén, "Genre and Countergenre: The Discovery of the Picaresque," in *Literature as a System*, 143.

14. Guillén, "Genre and Countergenre," 143. The eighteen editions that appear in WorldCat do not include the six editions of the spurious second part published from 1599 and 1605. Another six editions were published from 1695 to 1787.

15. Irving Leonard, *Books of the Brave: Being an Account of Books and of Men in the Spanish Conquest and Settlement of the Sixteenth-Century New World*, 2nd ed. (New York: Gordian, 1964), 259. Leonard based his conclusion largely on inventories of imported books inspected by officials of the Inquisition at the port of Veracruz.

16. "Bondad, inocencia, y fidelidad"; "que antes creyera dejarme hacer cien mil pedazos que cometer el más ligero crimen del mundo."

17. Dunn, *The Spanish Picaresque Novel*, 46.

18. He calls it "a master work matched only by Don Quixote": "una obra maestra, sólo comparable al Quijote." Michel Cavillac, *Guzmán de Alfarache y la novela moderna* (Madrid: Casa de Velásquez, 2010), 22.

19. Cavillac has much more to offer about Alemán's vision and the reach of this novel than I can summarize here, including the novelist's interest in scientific discoveries and inventions; money, bourgeois sensibilities, and the merchant capitalism of the time; political and pedagogical reforms; and the elimination of "sturdy beggars" in his moral scheme. (In England and elsewhere during the Early Modern Period, beggars were routinely suspected of feigning poverty and disabilities.) As Cavillac suggests, Alemán was not simply a conservative ideologue, and his novel is more than a religious apology.

20. WorldCat records four editions, in 1627, 1629 (2), and 1751. As with other early picaresque novels, the *reception* of *La vida del buscón* in the New World (or in Spain for that matter) has not been well documented.

21. Francisco de Quevedo, *Lazarillo de Tormes and The Grifter: Two Novels of the Low Life in Golden Age Spain*, trans. David Frye (Indianapolis: Hackett, 2015), 139. "Caballeros de rapiña." Francisco de Quevedo, *La vida del buscón*, ed. Fernando Cabo Aseguinolaza (Barcelona: Crítica, 1993), 170.

22. Quevedo, *Lazarillo de Tormes and The Grifter*, 61. "En mi mocedad siempre andaba por las iglesias y no de puro buen cristiano. Muchas veces me hubieran llorado en el asno si hubiera cantado en el potro. Nunca confesé sino cuando lo mandaba la Santa Madre Iglesia." Quevedo, *La vida del buscón*, 59.

23. "Las Indias"—the Indies—meant Spain's overseas possessions, another world of promise to Pablos more than a particular place. Quevedo chose not to say more about the destination, and never wrote the sequel he promised at the end of *La vida del buscón*.

24. Cruz, *Discourses of Poverty*, 198–206.

25. "Sólo pretendo con este pequeño volumen dar gusto a toda la nobleza." Estebanillo González, *La vida y hechos de Estebanillo González, hombre de buen humor,* compuesta por él mismo (Madrid: Espasa-Calpe, 1956), 46.

26. Cruz, *Discourses of Poverty,* 113; Maravall, *La literatura picaresca desde la historia social,* 6–7, 761. Maravall regards the literary *pícaros* as heroic figures in a time of economic, social, and historical crisis.

27. Cruz suggests that *Guzmán de Alfarache* would have been read in the eighteenth century for its entertaining picaresque stories, not for moral messages. Cruz, *Discourses of Poverty,* 198–206. Without direct evidence of reader response, it is hard to say. In *Gil Blas,* first published in 1715, Alain-René Lesage pointedly directed his readers to the moral lessons of his protagonist's adventures. Those lessons were expressed in secular terms, but not unlike Guzmán de Alfarache's warning: "Gentle Reader, whosoever you may be . . . if you peruse my adventures without paying attention to the moral instructions which they contain, you will derive no advantage from this work; but if you read it carefully, you will find in it, according to the precept of Horace, profit mingled with pleasure." Alain-René Lesage, *The Adventures of Gil Blas of Santillana,* trans. Henri Van Laun (Edinburgh: William Paterson, 1886), 1:lxii.

28. H. J. C. von Grimmelshausen, *The Adventures of Simplicius Simplicissimus,* trans. A. T. S. Goodrick (Lincoln: University of Nebraska Press, 1962), 373.

29. WorldCat records only a 1744 German edition for the eighteenth century, but the rise of Romanticism in the early nineteenth century made *Simplicius Simplicissimus* a hit again.

30. Just in the first two hundred entries in WorldCat, there are thirty-five editions before 1821 in French, thirty-six in English, eight in Spanish, four in German, three in Dutch, and one in Italian. Some of the English versions are plays, abridgements, and sequels. Not surprisingly, the English versions were published in London (twenty four), the United States (nine), Edinburgh (two), and Dublin (one), but the French editions were mostly published outside France. Thirteen were published in Paris and one in Rouen, but London accounts for twelve, Amsterdam three, and New York and Dublin one each.

31. Quoted in Dunn, *The Spanish Picaresque Novel,* 51.

32. "Las necedades y delirios de mi libertad, pereza y presunción." Diego de Torres Villarroel, *Vida, ascendencia, nacimiento, crianza y aventuras,* ed. Guy Mercadier (Madrid: Clásicos Castalia, 1972), 56, see also 49.

33. Especially Alexander Blackburn, *The Myth of the Picaro: Continuity and Transformation of the Picaresque Novel* (Chapel Hill: University of North Carolina Press, 1979). On tricksters more generally see Robert D. Pelton, *The Trickster in West Africa: A Study of Mythic Irony and Sacred Delight* (Berkeley: University of California Press, 1980); and Lewis Hyde's engaging book *Trickster Makes This World: How Disruptive Imagination Creates Culture* (Edinburgh: Canongate, 2008).

34. Their "personality is ambivalent and . . . [their] role equivocal." Mircea Eliade, *The Quest: History and Meaning in Religion* (Chicago: University of Chicago Press, 1968), 156. Jeanne Rosier Smith writes of tricksters as "endlessly multi-faceted and ambiguous." Jeanne Rosier Smith, *Writing Tricksters: Mythic Gambols in American Ethnic Fiction* (Berkeley: University of California Press, 1997), 7.

35. Hyde, *Trickster Makes This World*, 13. Hyde is helpful on much else about tricksters across cultures and time.

36. Guillén, "Toward a Definition of the Picaresque," 80, 88, 92, 96; Quevedo, *Lazarillo de Tormes and The Grifter*, 179.

37. Blackburn, *The Myth of the Picaro*, 7; Enrique Lamadrid, "The Rogue's Progress: Journeys of the Pícaro from Oral Tradition to Contemporary Chicano Literature of New Mexico," *MELUS* 20, no. 2 (Summer 1995): 15–24.

38. "En México lo picaresco se vive cada día como si fuese su lugar de origen." Javier Treviño Castro, "Síntoma de la urgente actualidad de la novela picaresca," *Vanguardia*, September 5, 2015, 1.

39. For the nineteenth century, Vicente Riva Palacio's Martín Garatuza is often also mentioned, and Riva Palacio even described him in protean terms as "una especie de Proteo, siempre en movimiento, siempre variando de forma" (a kind of Proteus, always in motion, always changing shape), but Garatuza is a cold-blooded highwayman with little of a *pícaro*'s nimble cunning and aversion to violence. Many picaresque characters, male and female, populate more recent Mexican literature, from José Rubén Romero's Pito Pérez in *La vida inútil de Pito Pérez* to Elena Poniatowska's Jesusa in *Hasta no verte, Jesús mío*.

40. "Sufría yo todas estas cosas porque por el amor que tenía a mi vida." Carlos de Sigüenza y Góngora, *Infortunios de Alonso Ramírez* (Mexico: Premia Editora, 1989), 52, my translation.

41. Most *relaciones de méritos* amount to abbreviated professional résumés, but several long narratives were written for the same purpose. For example,

Maese Joan's riveting account to the king of his eight years stranded on barren islets in the western Caribbean from 1528 to 1536 (Lesley Byrd Simpson, ed. and trans., "The Spanish Crusoe: An Account by Maese Joan of Eight Years Spent as a Castaway on the Serrana Keys in the Caribbean Sea, 1528–1536," *Hispanic American Historical Review* 9, no. 3 [August 1929]: 368–76); Alvar Núñez Cabeza de Vaca's account of his shipwreck on the coast of Florida and eight harrowing years wending his way through what would become the Spanish borderlands of North America (published first in 1542 as *Relación y comentarios*, later republished as *Naufragios*, literally "shipwrecks," but less literally "misfortunes"); and Bernal Díaz del Castillo's *Historia verdadera de la conquista de la Nueva España*, hoping to receive high honors for sacrifices and heroism in service to the king by men like himself during and after the conquest of Mexico.

42. "Quien dudará el que sea objeto de su munificencia en lo de adelante." Quoted in Timothy G. Compton, *Mexican Picaresque Narratives: Periquillo and Kin* (Lewisburg, PA: Bucknell University Press, 1997), 40.

43. As photographer Garry Winogrand supposedly put it, "When you put four edges around some facts, you change those facts."

44. Julie Greer Johnson thinks that the selection of narrative episodes—a poor young man striking out on his own, whose wife died young, who was taken captive on an ocean voyage, and who appealed to an advocation of the Virgin Mary—shows that Sigüenza knew the *Guzmán de Alfarache* text. Julie Greer Johnson, "Picaresque Elements in Carlos Sigüenza y Góngora's *Los Infortunios de Alonso Ramírez*," *Hispania* 64, no. 1 (March 1981): 60–67. Raquel Chang Rodríguez also sees Sigüenza as the creative author of the *Infortunios*, but as less influenced by Spanish picaresque novels and more forward-looking in his scientific and anthropological interests. Raquel Chang Rodríguez, "La transgresión de la picaresca en los *Infortunios de Alonso Ramírez*," in *Violencia y subversión en la prosa colonial hispanoamericana, siglos XVI y XVII* (Madrid: José Porrúa Turanzas, 1982), 85–108.

45. Patricio Boyer, "Criminality and Subjectivity in *Infortunios de Alonso Ramirez*," *Hispanic Review* 78, no. 1 (Winter 2010): 30. Two other examples of this view that the *Infortunios* is both Ramírez's story and Sigüenza's fiction of Ramírez's story are Aníbal González, "Los *Infortunios de Alonso Ramírez*: picaresca e historia," *Hispanic Review* 51, no. 2 (Spring 1983): 189–204; and Álvaro Félix Bolaños, "Sobre 'relaciones' e identidades en crisis: el 'Otro' lado del cautivo Alonso Ramírez," *Revista de Crítica Literaria Latinoamericana* 21,

no. 42 (1995): 131–60. Antonio Lorente Medina provides a helpful appraisal of the scholarly literature up to the mid-1990s, before it was certain that there had been a living, breathing Alonso Ramírez, in *La prosa de Sigüenza y Góngora y la formación de la conciencia criolla mexicana* (Mexico: Fondo de Cultura Económica, 1996), 163–75.

46. Fabio López Lázaro, "La mentira histórica de un pirata caribeño: el descubrimiento del transfondo histórico de los *Infortunios de Alonso Ramírez* (1690)," *Anuario de Estudios Americanos* 64, no. 2 (July–December 2007): 87–104; José F. Buscaglia-Salgado, "The History of the First American of Universal Standing: How Alonso Ramírez, a.k.a. Felipe Ferrer, Turned the World on Its Head by Circumnavigating the Globe," in *The Misfortunes of Alonso Ramírez (1690)*, ed. and trans. José F. Buscaglia-Salgado (New Brunswick, NJ: Rutgers University Press, 2019), 170. Correspondence between Viceroy Conde de Galve and his brother, the Spanish Duque del Infantado, shows that they were part of an aristocratic party that opposed Cardinal-Archbishop Portocarrero's sway at court and his vision for reform. Portocarrero wanted a greater share of the crown's share of Mexican silver sent back to Spain; Galve, as viceroy, sought to preserve the funds that had been designated for defense of New Spain's borders against French and English attacks. Ramírez's story of English piracy and abuse on the high seas was a gift to the viceroy and his party at court in Madrid. Buscaglia-Salgado avoids the term *pícaro* altogether when referring to Ramírez. For another recent article that makes an intriguing case for a different kind of creative role for Sigüenza y Góngora in the *Infortunios* text, see Boyer, "Criminality and Subjectivity in *Infortunios de Alonso Ramírez*," 25–48. Boyer argues that Sigüenza sought to examine "the role of early modern capitalism and maritime culture in the development of New World identities" (25).

47. José Joaquín Fernández de Lizardi, *The Mangy Parrot: The Life and Times of Periquillo Sarniento*, trans. David Frye (Indianapolis: Hackett, 2004), 372. "En primer lugar desterré a una muchacha bonita del pueblo porque vivía en incontinencia. Así sonó; pero el legítimo motivo fue porque no quiso condescender con mis solicitudes. . . . Después, mediante un regalito de trescientos pesos, acriminé a un pobre, cuyo principal delito era tener mujer bonita y sin honor. . . . A seguida requerí y amenacé a todos los que estaban incursos en el mismo delito, y ellos, temerosos de que no les desterrara a sus amadas, como lo sabía hacer, me pagaban las multas que quería. Tampoco dejé de anular las más formales escrituras. . . . Para coronar la obra, puse juego público en las

casas reales. . . . Una noche me dieron tal entrada, que no teniendo un real mío, descerrajé las cajas de comunidad y perdí todo el dinero que había en ellas." José Joaquín Fernández de Lizardi, *El Periquillo Sarniento (novela mexicana)* (Mexico: Ediciones Cicerón, n.d.), 255–56.

48. Fernández de Lizardi, *The Mangy Parrot*, 490. "Ni un muchacho bailador y atolondrado, sino un sacerdote sabio, ejemplar y circunspecto." Fernández de Lizardi, *El Periquillo Sarniento*, 329.

49. For an example of Fernández de Lizardi's view of the basic goodness of people see *The Mangy Parrot*, 515: "'Did you have a certain friend in jail whom you helped during the last days you were held?' 'Yes, I did,' he said; 'a poor lad known as Periquillo Sarniento, a well-born boy with a fine education, talents that were above the ordinary, and a good heart, who could well have become an upright man; but unfortunately for him, he had befriended a bunch of rogues, they had led him astray, and on account of them, he had ended up in that jail. . . . I realized that this boy Periquillo was bad because of the influence of his bad friends, rather than the wickedness in his heart, and so I was always convinced that, if he could be removed from those provocative enemies, he in himself would be rather inclined toward good.'" "'¿Tuvo usted algún amigo en la cárcel a quien socorrió en los últimos días de su prisión?' 'Sí, tuve,' me dijo, 'a un pobre joven, que era conocido por Periquillo Sarniento, muchacho bien nacido, de fina educación, de no vulgares talentos y de buen corazón harto dispuesto para haber sido hombre de bien; pero por desgracia se dió a la amistad de algunos pícaros, éstos lo pervirtieron, y por su causa se vió en aquella cárcel. . . . Yo conocí que el tal muchacho, Periquillo, era malo por el estímulo de sus malos amigos, más bien que por la malicia de su corazón, pues vivía persuadido de que, quitándole estos provocativos enemigos, él de por sí estaba bien dispuesto a la virtud.'" Fernández de Lizardi, *El Periquillo Sarniento*, 345–46. Picaresque novel or not, Fernández de Lizardi presents Periquillo as behaving like a *pícaro*. As Guillén puts it, "The *pícaro* can remain a *pícaro* while changing the ethical justification—the ideology—for his behavior." Guillén, "Toward a Definition of the Picaresque," 98.

50. In writings published from the 1930s to the 1950s, Jefferson Rea Spell emphasized Enlightenment interest in education reforms in Fernández de Lizardi's writings, especially in *El Periquillo Sarniento*. Jefferson Rea Spell, "The Intellectual Background of Lizardi as Reflected in *El Periquillo Sarniento*," *PMLA* 71, no. 3 (June 1956): 414–32; Jefferson Rea Spell, *The Life and Works of*

José Joaquín Fernández de Lizardi (Philadelphia: University of Pennsylvania Press, 1931); Jefferson Rea Spell, *Rousseau in the Spanish World before 1833: A Study in Franco-Spanish Literary Relations* (Austin: University of Texas Press, 1938), esp. 247. For more recent works focused on *El Periquillo Sarniento* as an Enlightenment text concerned with education reforms see Beatriz Alba Koch, *Ilustrando la Nueva España: Texto e imagen en "El Periquillo Sarniento" de Fernández de Lizardi* (Cáceres, Spain: Universidad de Extremadura, 1999); Jesús Hernández García, *Fernández de Lizardi: Un educador para un pueblo* (Mexico: UNAM, 2003). This is not the place for a lengthy discussion of the scholarly debate over whether *El Periquillo Sarniento* is or is not a picaresque novel. The debate follows lines similar to those in the scholarship on *Infortunios de Alonso Ramírez*, with most scholars offering a qualified no-but-yes answer: it has many elements of picaresque novels and shows a knowledge of that literature. Some critics consider *El Periquillo Sarniento* not picaresque because Cervantes is thought to be its main literary influence; for example John Skirius, "Fernández de Lizardi y Cervantes," *Nueva Revista de Filología Hispánica* 31, no. 2 (1982): 257–72; Javier Sánchez Zapatero, "Heterogeneidad y fuentes literarias de El Periquillo Sarniento de José Joaquín Fernández de Lizardi," *Espéculo. Revista de Estudios Literarios*, no. 34 (2007): http://webs.ucm.es/info/especulo /numero34/psarnien.html. For a recent interpretation of *El Periquillo Sarniento* as a picaresque novel see Emma Ramírez, "Ilustración y dominación: *El Periquillo Sarniento* bajo el Siglo de las Luces," *Revista de Humanidades: Tecnológico de Monterrey*, no. 21 (2006): 65–103. Ramírez sees the essence of the *pícaro* and *lo picaresco* as social marginality and insubordination. In her opinion, Periquillo's impersonations of colonial authorities and the ambiguities and ambivalences in the language he and other marginalized characters of the novel use become subversions of Bourbon tyranny. She regards *pícaros* as masters of ambiguous "lenguajes ocultos," wielding what James Scott calls "weapons of the weak."

51. Fernández de Lizardi, *The Mangy Parrot*, 499, 530. "Soy tu amigo y lo seré siempre que me honres con tu amistad"; "hay muchos amigos, pero pocas amistades. Amigos sobran en el tiempo favorable; pero pocos o ningunos en el adverso." Fernández de Lizardi, *El Periquillo Sarniento*, 335, 355.

52. Beristáin de Souza considered Fernández de Lizardi an original talent, an "ingenious original who, if he had added to his efforts a greater knowledge of the world of men and a better choice of books, would merit, if not the title of

the American Quevedo, at least that of the Mexican Torres Villarroel": "ingenio original que si hubiese añadido a su aplicación más conocimiento del mundo de los hombres y mejor elección de libros, podría merecer si no el nombre de Quevedo americano, a lo menos el de Torres Villarroel mexicano." About *El Periquillo Sarniento* he says, "Based on what I have seen of it, it is similar to the [novel] of *Guzmán de Alfarache*": "que según lo he visto de ella, tiene semejanza con la del *Guzmán de Alfarache.*" José Mariano Beristáin de Souza, *Biblioteca Hispano-Americana septentrional o catalogo y noticia de los literatos...* (Mexico: Ediciones Fuente Cultural, 1947), vol. 2, tomo III, 129.

53. Fernández de Lizardi, *The Mangy Parrot*, 494, 521. "Los justos en esta expresión del santo David, deben alegrarse y regocijarse en el Señor"; "vuestra madre quedó inconsolable con tal pérdida y necesitó valerse de todos las consideraciones con que nos alivia en tales lances la religión católica, que puede ministrar auxilios sólidos a los verdaderos dolientes." Fernández de Lizardi, *El Periquillo Sarniento*, 332, 350.

54. Fernández de Lizardi, *The Mangy Parrot*, 488–92, 530–33.

55. "The priest was fairly well educated: a doctor in canon law, he avoided all scandalous behavior and was polite to a fault; but these fine qualities were tarnished by his sordid self-interest and his pronounced greed. As you can imagine, he had no sense of charity; and as everyone knows, where that solid foundation is lacking, the beautiful edifice of virtue can never be built." Fernández de Lizardi, *The Mangy Parrot*, 367. "Él era bastante instruído, doctor en Cánones, nada escandaloso y demasiado atento: mas estas prendas se deslucían con su sórdido interés y declarada codicia. Ya se deja entender que no tenía caridad, y se sabe que donde falta este sólido cimiento no puede fabricarse el hermoso edificio de las virtudes." Fernández de Lizardi, *El Periquillo Sarniento*, 252.

56. Fernández de Lizardi, *The Mangy Parrot*, 367. "Hombre de bello genio, virtuoso sin hipocresía." Fernández de Lizardi, *El Periquillo Sarniento*, 253. For Fernández de Lizardi's exemplary priests see *The Mangy Parrot*, chapters 27 and 34, and p. 367 for the priest of Chilapa.

57. Fernández de Lizardi, *The Mangy Parrot*, 503 (repeated on 511), 530. "De ninguna manera conviene dejarlo en este estado. La humanidad y la religión nos mandan socorrerlo. Hagámoslo"; "amad y honrad a Dios y observad sus preceptos." Fernández de Lizardi, *El Periquillo Sarniento*, 337, 355. "God is still here to comfort you and aid you, and if you fulfill His divine precepts and trust

in His high Providence, you may be sure that you will never lack for anything, anything at all, to make you happy in this life and the next." Fernández de Lizardi, *The Mangy Parrot*, 529. "Dios os queda para favoreceros y ampararos, y si cumplís sus divinos preceptos y confiáis en su altísima Providencia, estad seguros de que nada, nada os faltará para ser felices en esta y en la otra vida." Fernández de Lizardi, *El Periquillo Sarniento*, 355.

58. "The idiot is still waiting for me": "la zonza aún me estará aguardando." José Joaquín Fernández de Lizardi, *Vida y hechos del famoso caballero D. Catrín de la Fachenda* (Mexico: Alejandro Valdés, 1832), 125.

59. "Buscar la vida sin vergüenza." Fernández de Lizardi, *Vida y hechos del famoso caballero D. Catrín de la Fachenda*, 123.

60. "Son hombres de bien, hombres decentes, y sobre todo, nobles y caballeros." José Joaquín Fernández de Lizardi, *Don Catrín de la Fachenda y noches tristes y día alegre*, 7th ed. (Mexico: Editorial Porrúa, 1989), 63.

61. "Vivió mal, murió lo mismo." Fernández de Lizardi, *Vida y hechos del famoso caballero D. Catrín de la Fachenda*, 152. In Compton's estimation, for these reasons *Don Catrín de la Fachenda* "most closely resembles the ideal picaresque model" of the works he studied. Compton, *Mexican Picaresque Narratives*, 127. For a close study and somewhat different reading of *Don Catrín de la Fachenda* see Nancy Vogeley, *Lizardi and the Birth of the Novel in Spanish America* (Gainesville: University Press of Florida, 2001), 237-44.

62. Dale Shuger notes that wanderlust was taken as a symptom of madness. Dale Shuger, *Don Quixote in the Archives: Madness and Literature in Early Modern Spain* (Edinburgh: Edinburgh University Press, 2012), 42.

Chapter Four

1. "Pablos, abre el ojo, que asan carne. Mira por ti, que aquí no tienes otro padre, ni madre." Francisco de Quevedo, *La vida del buscón*, ed. Fernando Cabo Aseguinolaza (Barcelona: Crítica, 1993), 88, my translation.

2. Francisco de Quevedo, *Lazarillo de Tormes and The Grifter: Two Novels of the Low Life in Golden Age Spain*, trans. David Frye (Indianapolis: Hackett, 2015), 59. "Descendiente[s] de la gloria," Quevedo, *La vida del buscón*, 55.

3. Claudio Guillén, "Toward a Definition of the Picaresque," in *Literature as a System: Essays toward the Theory of Literary History* (Princeton, NJ: Princeton University Press, 1971), 76.

4. José Joaquín Fernández de Lizardi, *The Mangy Parrot: The Life and Times of Periquillo Sarniento*, trans. David Frye (Indianapolis: Hackett, 2004), 350. "Si todos los hombres dieran al público sus vidas escritas con la sencillez y exactitud que yo, aparecerían una multitud de Periquillos en el mundo; cuyos altos y bajos, favorables y adversas se nos esconden porque cada uno procura ocultarnos sus deslices." José Joaquín Fernández de Lizardi, *El Periquillo Sarniento (novela mexicana)* (Mexico: Ediciones Cicerón, n.d.), 241-42. He makes this point again on pp. 469 and 529 of *The Mangy Parrot*. Spanish academic and literary figure Diego de Torres Villarroel wrote in much the same way in the early eighteenth century: "We're all the same and, with minor differences, each one as bad as the rest": "todos somos unos y, con corta diferencia, tan malos los unos como los otros." Diego de Torres Villarroel, *Vida, ascendencia, nacimiento, crianza y aventuras*, ed. Guy Mercadier (Madrid: Clásicos Castalia, 1972), 54-55.

5. Natalie Z. Davis, *The Return of Martin Guerre* (Cambridge, MA: Harvard University Press, 1983), 36-37.

6. Miguel de Cervantes, *Don Quixote*, trans. Edith Grossman (New York: HarperCollins, 2003), 161. "Dixo Sancho que yo Christiano viejo soy, y para ser Conde esto me basta." Miguel de Cervantes Saavedra, *El ingenioso hidalgo Don Quixote de la Mancha* (Madrid: Juan de la Cuesta, 1605), vol. 1, part 3, ch. 21, fol. 99v.

7. Cited in Ramón Menéndez Pidal, *The Spaniards in Their History*, trans. Walter Starkie (London: Hollis and Carter, 1950), 122.

8. Américo Castro, *The Structure of Spanish History*, trans. Edmund L. King (Princeton, NJ: Princeton University Press, 1954), 631 (the exact numbers cited are 108,358 out of 889,940); Ignacio Atienza Hernández, "'Refeudalisation' in Castile during the Seventeenth Century: A Cliché?," in *The Castilian Crisis of the Seventeenth Century: New Perspectives on the Economic and Social History of Seventeenth-Century Spain*, ed. I. A. A. Thompson and Bartolomé Yun Casaslilla (Cambridge, UK: Cambridge University Press, 1994), 255.

9. John A. Crow, *Spain: The Root and the Flower: An Interpretation of Spain and the Spanish People* (Berkeley: University of California Press, 1985), 159-60; Menéndez Pidal, *The Spaniards in Their History*, 122, 153; Castro, *The Structure of Spanish History*, 628-35; Américo Castro, *The Spaniards: An Introduction to Their History*, trans. Willard F. King and Selma Margaretten (Berkeley: University of California Press, 1971), 67, 126, 271, 457. Castro and the others risked reducing notions of status and tradition to timeless features of national

character, labor, and economic development. Ruth MacKay dismantles for Early Modern Spain the idea that manual labor was in any simple sense dishonorable and that Spain was a land of idlers in *"Lazy, Improvident People": Myth and Reality in the Writing of Spanish History* (Ithaca, NY, and London: Cornell University Press, 2006).

10. Crow, *Spain*, 159–60. Sancho Panza put it this way: "Though I'm poor I'm an Old Christian, and I don't owe anything to anybody. . . . Not all Pedros are the same": "aunque pobre soy Christiano viejo, y no debo nada a nadie . . ., y algo va de Pedro a Pedro." Cervantes Saavedra, *El ingenioso hidalgo Don Quixote de la Mancha*, vol. 1, part 4, ch. 47, fol. 288r, my translation.

11. Fernández de Lizardi, *The Mangy Parrot*, 392–93. "La mendiga de una fortuna accidental"; "todo el mundo sabe que la gente minera es por lo regular viciosa, provocativa, soberbia y desperdiciada." Fernández de Lizardi, *El Periquillo Sarniento*, 268, 269.

12. I have left Sigüenza's *Infortunios de Alonso Ramírez* out of this discussion although some readers regard Ramírez as a picaresque figure and Sigüenza's account as a contribution to picaresque literature. Aguayo and Ramírez had in common their vagabond, homeless young adulthood and their will to escape impoverishment and overcome many hardships—in a word, their will to live and get ahead ("subir a más") even in a corrupt world. But unlike Aguayo, by this account Ramírez is resolutely hardworking, honest, and pious.

13. "Que tenía cara de hombre agudo y de buen entendimiento." Quevedo, *La vida del buscón*, 60, my translation.

14. Quevedo, *Lazarillo de Tormes and The Grifter*, 138, 118. "Tanto que aun por descuido no decía verdad"; "el deseo de verme entre gente principal y caballeros." Quevedo, *La vida del buscón*, 169, 138.

15. Francisco de Quevedo, *Lazarillo de Tormes and The Swindler (El Buscón): Two Spanish Picaresque Novels*, trans. Michael Alpert (London: Penguin, 2003), 121. "Allá quedarás, bellaco, deshonra-buenos, jinete de gaznates." Quevedo, *La vida del buscón*, 140.

16. Peter N. Dunn, *The Spanish Picaresque Novel* (Boston: Twayne, 1979), 49.

17. From James Tate, "Consumed" (1991), in *Selected Poems* (Hanover, NH: University Press of New England for Wesleyan University Press, 1991), 50, copyright James Tate, used by permission.

18. "Parcos en el comer, y sobrios en el beber, pero superfluos en el vestir." Baltasar Gracián, *Obras de Lorenzo Gracián. Tomo primero, que contiene el*

Criticón, primera, segunda, y tercera parte. El Oráculo, y Héroe (Barcelona: Imprenta de María Ángeles Martí y Galí, 1757), 165.

19. Quevedo, *Lazarillo de Tormes and The Grifter*, 172. "Púseme el vestido con que solía hacer los galanes en las comedias." Quevedo, *La vida del buscón*, 216.

20. Quevedo, *Lazarillo de Tormes and The Grifter*, 121. "Que hay tanto que ver en mí como tengo porque nada cubro." Quevedo, *La vida del buscón*, 142.

21. William Barker, ed., *The Adages of Erasmus* (Toronto: University of Toronto Press, 2001), 240.

22. Joel Paris, *The Bipolar Spectrum: Diagnosis or Fad?* (New York and London: Routledge, 2012), 82–83. Andre F. Carvalho and Edward Vieta estimate that 2 percent of the general population in the United States suffers from a bipolar disorder, and that relapses are common. Andre F. Carvalho and Edward Vieta, eds., *The Treatment of Bipolar Disorder: Integrative Clinical Strategies and Future Directions* (Oxford and New York: Cambridge University Press, 2017), 157.

23. Paris, *The Bipolar Spectrum*, 13; Gin S. Malhi and Yulisha Byrow, "The Current Classification of Bipolar Disorders," in *The Treatment of Bipolar Disorder*, 5.

24. Bassey Ikpi, "What Bipolar II Feels Like," *New York Times*, July 6, 2019, Opinion section, https://www.nytimes.com/2019/07/06/opinion/sunday/bipolar-bassey-ikpi-book.html.

25. Atondo did not present a dramatic breakdown like Bartolomé Sánchez's incoherent ravings and blasphemies in the parish church of Cardenete, Spain, during services one Sunday in 1552. But even Sánchez was not quickly judged demented or in thrall to the Devil by the Inquisitors who heard the cases of heresy against him, although his behavior became increasingly bizarre, and his claim to be a new messiah, the prophet Elijah sent by God to avenge Christ's death, could not be ignored. At fifty-one—old for the time—he had led an inconspicuous life until then as a farmer and then a wool carder and day laborer after he was forced to give up farming around 1550. And he remained a good worker and fluent storyteller despite his strange, heretical claims and talk of visions. He was tried twice for heresy—a second conviction would have meant certain death—but the Inquisitor in the second trial was convinced Sánchez had lost his mind and accepted the defense attorney's argument for temporary insanity. After the second trial, Sánchez was ordered flogged for burning his *sanbenito* (penitent's bib), and then released. If Sánchez had attracted a following, the outcome might have been different. Whether he was

eventually institutionalized is not clear from the record. Sara Nalle, *Mad for God: Bartolomé Sánchez, the Secret Messiah of Cardenete* (Charlottesville: University Press of Virginia, 2001). Like Sánchez, Atondo spoke of his "congoja" (anguish), and both men claimed to have had a vision that marked their sense of religious mission. Dale Shuger discusses other Spanish Inquisition cases from the sixteenth and seventeenth centuries in which the tribunal judged the accused mad or otherwise incapacitated mentally and emotionally, and issued a lenient sentence, such as a year of seclusion in a monastery. Dale Shuger, *Don Quixote in the Archives: Madness and Literature in Early Modern Spain* (Edinburgh: Edinburgh University Press, 2012), 42–63.

26. Roy Porter, *Madness: A Brief History* (Oxford: Oxford University Press, 2002), 45–48. For a sweeping, authoritative study of depression and other dejected states in Western medical thought and practice across two millennia, there is Stanley W. Jackson, *Melancholia and Depression: From Hippocratic Times to Modern Times* (New Haven, CT: Yale University Press, 1986). Jackson notes the long association of melancholia and mania on pp. 385–86, which became closer than ever in the early twentieth century thanks to German psychiatrist Emil Kraepelin's classification of mental illness.

27. "Soledad radical del pícaro." José Antonio Maravall, *La literatura picaresca desde la historia social (siglos XVI y XVII)* (Madrid: Taurus, 1986), 317.

28. "Que la cosa que más me consolaba que había de valerme por mi habilidad." Quevedo, *La vida del buscón*, 140, my translation. A similar statement in Sigüenza's *Infortunios de Alonso Ramírez* also follows the plotline of some early Spanish picaresque novels: "I decided to leave my homeland in order to seek greater advantages in foreign places": "determiné hurtarle el cuerpo a mi misma patria para buscar en las ajenas más conveniencia." Carlos de Sigüenza y Góngora, *Infortunios de Alonso Ramírez* (Mexico: Premia Editora, 1989), 17, my translation.

29. "Con el ánimo de buscar mi vida . . . por vien o por mal." See chapter 1, note 1.

30. In eighteenth-century judicial records, the word *pícaro* usually meant scoundrel, as it did when a provocative peninsular Spaniard silversmith living in Veracruz spoke ill of priests: "He treats priests as *pícaros* and rascals the same as any other person, whether or not they are honorable": "que a los sacerdotes los trata de pícaros y brebiones, igualmente que a qualquiera otra

persona, sea, or no sea de honor." Huntington Library HM35180, trial of Miguel de Zaragoza, 1780–1782.

Conclusion

1. Inga Clendinnen, "Norman Mailer Meets Jack Ruby," *Heat 7* (1998): 49–55. Used by permission of Giramondo Publishing Co.

2. See Stuart B. Schwartz, *All Can Be Saved: Religious Tolerance and Salvation in the Iberian Atlantic World* (New Haven, CT: Yale University Press, 2008), 12, 42, 125, 212, 237 and elsewhere. Schwartz suggests that freedom of conscience was widespread among ordinary Catholics in Spain and Spanish America at the time.

3. For Clendinnen's views on metaphors people live by see Inga Clendinnen, Australian Biography interview, 2000, tape 12, p. 2, accessed online at https://australianbiography.gov.au/subjects/clendinnen/scripttext.html.

4. Erving Goffman, *The Presentation of Self in Everyday Life* (New York: Anchor, 1959), 17.

5. Gary Lindberg, *The Confidence Man in American Literature* (New York: Oxford University Press, 1982), 4.

6. Lindberg, *The Confidence Man*, 9. Here Lindberg compares *pícaros* to confidence men and makes this distinction. He tracks the emergence of the confidence man as ambivalent hero in US culture and literature to the turbulent years before the Civil War, from the trial of William Thompson in late 1849 to publication of P. T. Barnum's autobiography in 1855 and Melville's novel *The Confidence Man: His Masquerade* in 1857.

7. David Sinclair, *The Land That Never Was: Sir Gregor MacGregor and the Most Audacious Fraud in History* (Cambridge, MA: Da Capo, 2003). Free of footnotes, this book offers an eventful narrative of MacGregor's schemes, swindles, and military endeavors. Sinclair relies heavily on the promotional literature for Poyais, MacGregor's spiel, and the harsh appraisal by his contemporary, Colonel Michael Rafter. MacGregor himself remains a specter in these sources and the secondary literature. Specter or not, there is more to his story than the maneuverings of a self-made charlatan. He was enmeshed in a wider world of foreign land speculation and colonization schemes in early nineteenth-century Latin America and especially in the efforts of British

merchants and bankers to profit from commerce, industry, and mining in the new nations.

8. Javier Cercas, *The Impostor: A True Story*, trans. Frank Wynne (New York: Alfred A. Knopf, 2018), 20. In Cercas's Spanish, "(de vez en cuando Marco pasaba de la primera a la tercera persona, igual que si no hablase de sí mismo): él era un gran hombre, una persona generosa y solidaria y muy humana, un luchador incansable por las buenas causas, y por eso tanta gente decía maravillas de él." Javier Cercas, *El impostor* (Barcelona: Literatura Random House, 2014), 36.

9. Cercas, *The Impostor*, 349, 412.

10. In his fantasies of success, power, and brilliance, grandiose sense of self-importance, and constant need for adulation, Marco has less in common with Atondo or Aguayo than he does with Robert Parkin Peters, the boundlessly, criminally deceitful English cleric and academic whom Adam Sisman considers a "textbook case" of narcissistic personality disorder. Adam Sisman, *The Professor and the Parson: A Story of Desire, Deceit, and Defrocking* (Berkeley: Counterpoint, 2020), 203-4.

11. Mario Vargas Llosa, "The Man Who Wasn't There" (book review of Javier Cercas's *The Impostor*), *Wall Street Journal*, August 28, 2018, https://www.wsj.com/articles/the-impostor-review-the-man-who-wasnt-there-1535060707.

12. Most recently proposed by Malcolm Gladwell in *Talking to Strangers: What We Should Know About the People We Don't Know* (New York: Allen Lane, 2019). Gladwell relies on the research of Timothy R. Levine in *Duped: Truth-Default Theory and the Social Science of Lying and Deception* (Tuscaloosa: University of Alabama Press, 2019).

13. The two positions touched on here just scratch the surface of the meaning of liberty in the eighteenth century. In the vast literature on liberty, this probing essay is still a good starting point: Isaiah Berlin, "Two Concepts of Liberty," in *Four Essays on Liberty* (New York: Oxford University Press, 1969), 118-72.

14. On the radical side of the Enlightenment as a profound revolution of the mind see Jonathan I. Israel, *Radical Enlightenment: Philosophy and the Making of Modernity, 1650-1750* (New York: Oxford University Press, 2002); Peter Gay, *The Enlightenment*, 2 vols. (New York: W.W. Norton, 1995, 1996); Ernst Cassirer, *The Philosophy of the Enlightenment* (Princeton, NJ: Princeton University Press, 1951).

15. "Yo vivía en las leyes escritas por los Santos Padres y no en las de ahora, que están imponiendo los hombres díscolos en entregados al libertinaje." See chapter 2, note 1.

16. A few days before, the bishop-elect of Michoacán ordered Morelos to post a notice on the parish church door announcing Hidalgo's excommunication. That led Morelos to visit Hidalgo and inquire about his movement. Apparently Morelos offered to serve as a chaplain, but was persuaded by Hidalgo to accept a military commission. Wilbert H. Timmons, *Morelos: Priest, Soldier, Statesman of Mexico* (El Paso: Texas Western College Press, 1963), 40. Niall Ferguson argues that social networks "are the true drivers of change," more than the hierarchical institutions of states, armies, and corporations, especially after the introduction of the printing press to Europe in the late fifteenth century up until the end of the eighteenth century, and again in our own time, since the 1970s. Niall Ferguson, *The Square and the Tower: Networks and Power, from the Freemasons to Facebook* (New York: Penguin, 2018), dust jacket, xxv. True or not in these stark terms, horizontal networks of communication mixed with, and sometimes challenged, the hierarchies of colonial authority in Mexico in ways that raised some unlikely individuals to prominence and power.

17. As networkers and prospective rebels, Aguayo and Atondo stand in contrast to the bandit gangs—groups of five, ten, sometimes fifty or so—that increasingly preyed on travelers and ranches in central and western Mexico during the late eighteenth century. In the independence wars, some members of these gangs temporarily made common cause with insurgent groups through personal contacts, chance meetings, and the promise of plunder. These highwaymen and cattle rustlers were part of a growing, mobile underworld of criminals that reached from rural areas to cities. The gang members were violent young men on horseback, in their late twenties and thirties, most of them illiterate, and many of them wanted for assault, murder, armed robbery, escaping from prison, desertion from the royal army, contraband trade, or attacks on rural estates. They came together more by chance than by design, often without a definite leader, but usually with a core group of family members. They met up at regional fairs, especially the Feria de San Juan de los Lagos in eastern Jalisco, or in cities where their booty could more easily be fenced. Local authorities were their natural foes, but whenever a local mayor protected the gangs, their network grew. For a regional study of bandit gangs in the late eighteenth

century and independence period see William B. Taylor, "Bandolerismo e insurgencia en el centro de Jalisco, 1790–1816," *Encuentro: Ciencias Sociales y Humanidades* 1, no. 3 (April–June 1984): 5–54.

18. Francisco de Quevedo, *Lazarillo de Tormes and The Grifter: Two Novels of the Low Life in Golden Age Spain*, trans. David Frye (Indianapolis: Hackett, 2015), 179. "Determiné . . . de pasarme a Indias . . . a ver si mudando mundo y tierra mejoraría mi suerte. Y fueme peor, . . . pues nunca mejora su estado quien muda solamente de lugar, y no de vida y costumbres." Francisco de Quevedo, *La vida del buscón*, ed. Fernando Cabo Aseguinolaza (Barcelona: Crítica, 1993), 226.

19. "Vi tan perdida la Fee Católica que esto me movió hazer lo que he hecho y si con hazer un exemplar con mi persona se remedia, pronto estoi resignado a sufrir todo quanto sea de agrado de Dios y de VS Yllma."

20. José Joaquín Fernández de Lizardi, *The Mangy Parrot: The Life and Times of Periquillo Sarniento*, trans. David Frye (Indianapolis: Hackett, 2004), 521. "Pasado este cruel invierno, todo ha sido primavera, viviendo juntos vuestra madre, yo, y vosotros, y disfrutando de una paz y de unos placeres inocentes, en una medianía honrada, que sin abastecerme para superfluidades, me ha dado todo lo necesario para no desear la suerte de los señores ricos y potentados." José Joaquín Fernández de Lizardi, *El Periquillo Sarniento (novela mexicana)* (Mexico: Ediciones Cicerón, n.d.), 350.

Works Cited

Manuscripts

Archivo General de la Nación (Mexico), Ramo Inquisición
    Vol. 1078 exp. 13
    Vol. 1096 exp. 9
    Vol. 1172 exp. 12
    Vol. 1376 exp. 6
    Vol. 1421 exp. 24
Bancroft Library, University of California, Berkeley, Mss 96-95m, vol. 23
Biblioteca Nacional, Madrid, Mss #2449-50
Huntington Library, San Marino, California, HM35180
Inga Clendinnen, Australian Biography interview, 2000, accessed online at
    https://australianbiography.gov.au/subjects/clendinnen/scripttext.html

Printed materials

Abercrombie, Thomas A. *Passing to América: Antonio (Née María) Yta's Transgressive, Transatlantic Life in the Twilight of the Spanish Empire.* University Park, PA: Penn State University Press, 2018.

Alba Koch, Beatriz. *Ilustrando la Nueva España: Texto e imagen en "El Periquillo Sarniento" de Fernández de Lizardi.* Cáceres, Spain: Universidad de Extremadura, 1999.

Alemán, Mateo. *Guzmán de Alfarache.* 2 vols. Madrid: Cátedra, 1984.

Anonymous. *La vida de Lazarillo de Tormes*. Edited by H. J. Chaytor. Manchester: Manchester University Press, 1922.

———. *Lazarillo de Tormes and The Grifter: Two Novels of the Low Life in Golden Age Spain*. Translated by David Frye. Indianapolis: Hackett, 2015.

———. *Lazarillo de Tormes and The Swindler (El Buscón): Two Spanish Picaresque Novels*. Translated by Michael Alpert. London: Penguin, 2003.

Atienza Hernández, Ignacio. "'Refeudalisation' in Castile during the Seventeenth Century: A Cliché?." In *The Castilian Crisis of the Seventeenth Century: New Perspectives on the Economic and Social History of Seventeenth-Century Spain*, edited by I. A. A. Thompson and Bartolomé Yun Casaslilla, 249–74. Cambridge, UK: Cambridge University Press, 1994.

Bancroft, Hubert Howe. *History of Mexico*. 6 vols. San Francisco: Bancroft, 1883–88.

Barker, William, ed. *The Adages of Erasmus*. Toronto: University of Toronto Press, 2001.

Bennassar, Bartolomé. *Recherches sur les grandes épidémies dans le nord de l'Espagne à la fin du XVIe siècle*. Problèmes de documentation et de méthode. Paris: SEVPEN, 1969.

Bergamo, Ilarione da. *Daily Life in Colonial Mexico: The Journey of Friar Ilarione da Bergamo*. Edited by Robert Ryall Miller and William J. Orr. Translated by William J. Orr. Norman: University of Oklahoma Press, 2000.

Beristáin de Souza, José Mariano. *Biblioteca Hispano-Americana septentrional o catálogo y noticia de los literatos . . .* 2 vols. Mexico: Ediciones Fuente Cultural, 1947.

Berlin, Isaiah. *Four Essays on Liberty*. New York: Oxford University Press, 1969.

Blackburn, Alexander. *The Myth of the Picaro: Continuity and Transformation of the Picaresque Novel*. Chapel Hill: University of North Carolina Press, 1979.

Bolaños, Álvaro Félix. "Sobre 'relaciones' e identidades en crisis: el 'Otro' lado del cautivo Alonso Ramírez." *Revista de Crítica Literaria Latinoamericana* 21, no. 42 (1995): 131–60.

Boyer, Patricio. "Criminality and Subjectivity in *Infortunios de Alonso Ramírez*." *Hispanic Review* 78, no. 1 (Winter 2010): 25–48.

Boyer, Richard. *Lives of the Bigamists: Marriage, Family, and Community in Colonial Mexico*. Albuquerque: University of New Mexico Press, 1995.

Buscaglia-Salgado, José F. "The History of the First American of Universal Standing: How Alonso Ramírez, a.k.a. Felipe Ferrer, Turned the World on Its Head by Circumnavigating the Globe." In Carlos de Sigüenza y Góngora, *The Misfortunes of Alonso Ramírez (1690)*, edited and translated by José F. Buscaglia-Salgado, 161–226. New Brunswick, NJ: Rutgers University Press, 2019.

Campbell, Joseph. *The Hero with a Thousand Faces*. Princeton, NJ: Princeton University Press, 1949.

Carvalho, Andre F., and Edward Vieta, eds. *The Treatment of Bipolar Disorder: Integrative Clinical Strategies and Future Directions*. Cambridge, UK, and New York: Cambridge University Press, 2017.

Cassirer, Ernst. *The Philosophy of the Enlightenment*. Princeton, NJ: Princeton University Press, 1951.

Castro, Américo. *The Spaniards: An Introduction to Their History*. Translated by Willard F. King and Selma Margaretten. Berkeley: University of California Press, 1971.

———. *The Structure of Spanish History*. Translated by Edmund L. King. Princeton, NJ: Princeton University Press, 1954.

Cavillac, Michel. *Guzmán de Alfarache y la novela moderna*. Madrid: Casa de Velásquez, 2010.

Cercas, Javier. *El impostor*. Barcelona: Literatura Random House, 2014.

———. *The Impostor: A True Story*. Translated by Frank Wynne. New York: Alfred A. Knopf, 2018.

Cervantes, Miguel de. *Don Quixote*. Translated by Edith Grossman. New York: HarperCollins, 2003.

Cervantes Saavedra, Miguel de. *El ingenioso hidalgo Don Quixote de la Mancha*. 2 vols. Madrid: Juan de la Cuesta, 1605, 1615.

Chang Rodríguez, Raquel. "La transgresión de la picaresca en *Los Infortunios de Alonso Ramírez*." In *Violencia y subversión en la prosa colonial hispanoamericana, siglos XVI y XVII*, 85–108. Madrid: José Porrúa Turanzas, 1982.

Chuchiak, John F. *The Inquisition in New Spain, 1536–1820: A Documentary History*. Baltimore: Johns Hopkins University Press, 2012.

Clendinnen, Inga. "Norman Mailer Meets Jack Ruby." *Heat 7* (1998): 49–55.

Cobarruvias, Sebastián de. *Tesoro de la lengua castellana o española*. Madrid: Ediciones Turner, 1984. Originally published 1610.

Coll Tellechea, Reyes. *Lazarillo castigado: Historia de un olvido*. Madrid: Ediciones del Orto; Minneapolis: University of Minnesota Press, 2010.

Compton, Timothy G. *Mexican Picaresque Narratives: Periquillo and Kin*. Lewisburg, PA: Bucknell University Press, 1997.

Corteguera, Luis. *Death by Effigy: A Case from the Mexican Inquisition*. Philadelphia: University of Pennsylvania Press, 2012.

Crow, John A. *Spain: The Root and the Flower. An Interpretation of Spain and the Spanish People*. Berkeley: University of California Press, 1985.

Cruz, Anne J. *Discourses of Poverty: Social Reform and the Picaresque Novel in Early Modern Spain*. Toronto: University of Toronto Press, 1999.

Davis, Natalie Z. *The Return of Martin Guerre*. Cambridge, MA: Harvard University Press, 1983.

Díaz Plaja, Fernando. *The Spaniard and the Seven Deadly Sins*. Translated by John Inderwick Palmer. New York: Charles Scribner's Sons, 1967.

Diccionario de la lengua castellana, por La Academia Española. 6th ed. Madrid: La Imprenta Nacional, 1822.

Dunn, Peter N. *Spanish Picaresque Fiction: A New Literary History*. Ithaca, NY: Cornell University Press, 1993.

———. *The Spanish Picaresque Novel*. Boston: Twayne, 1979.

Eliade, Mircea. *The Quest: History and Meaning in Religion*. Chicago: University of Chicago Press, 1968.

Eliav-Feldon, Miriam. *Renaissance Impostors and Proofs of Identity*. New York: Palgrave Macmillan, 2012.

Feitler, Bruno. "The Inquisition Brotherhood: Cofradía de San Pedro Mártir of Colonial Mexico." *The Americas* 40, no. 2 (October 1983): 171–207.

Ferguson, Niall. *The Square and the Tower: Networks and Power, from the Freemasons to Facebook*. New York: Penguin, 2018.

Fernández de Lizardi, José Joaquín. *Don Catrín de la Fachenda y noches tristes y día alegre*. 7th ed. Mexico: Editorial Porrúa, 1989.

———. *El Periquillo Sarniento (novela mexicana)*. Mexico: Ediciones Cicerón, n.d. [1940s?].

———. *The Mangy Parrot: The Life and Times of Periquillo Sarniento*. Translated by David Frye. Indianapolis: Hackett, 2004.

———. *Vida y hechos del famoso caballero D. Catrín de la Fachenda*. Mexico: Alejandro Valdés, 1832.

Gay, Peter. *The Enlightenment.* 2 vols. New York: W.W. Norton, 1995, 1996.

Gladwell, Malcolm. *Talking to Strangers: What We Should Know about the People We Don't Know.* New York: Allen Lane, 2019.

Glesener, Thomas. "Se (re)faire musulman. L'accès des pauvres intinérants aux droits de la conversion (Espagne, XVIIIe siècle)." *Revue d'histoire moderne et contemporaine* 64, no. 2 (April–June 2017): 129–56.

Goffman, Erving. *The Presentation of Self in Everyday Life.* New York: Anchor, 1959.

González, Aníbal. "*Los Infortunios de Alonso Ramírez*: picaresca e historia." *Hispanic Review* 51, no. 2 (Spring 1983): 189–204.

González, Estebanillo. *La vida y hechos de Estebanillo González, hombre de buen humor, compuesta por él mismo.* Madrid: Espasa-Calpe, 1956.

Gordian, Michael. "The Culture of Dis/simulation in Sixteenth- and Seventeenth-Century Europe." PhD thesis, Warburg Institute, University of London, 2014.

Gracián, Baltasar. *Obras completas.* Edited by Miguel Batllori and Ceferino Peralta. Madrid: Atlas, 1969.

———. *Obras de Lorenzo Gracián. Tomo primero, que contiene El Criticón, primera, segunda, y tercera parte. El oráculo, y héroe.* Barcelona: Imprenta de María Ángeles Martí y Galí, 1757.

Greene, Graham. *The Power and the Glory.* London: William Heinemann, 1940.

Greenleaf, Richard E. "The Inquisition Brotherhood: Cofradía de San Pedro Mártir of Colonial Mexico." *The Americas* 40, no. 2 (October 1983): 171–207.

———. "The Inquisition in Eighteenth-Century New Mexico." *New Mexico Historical Review* 60, no. 1 (January 1985): 29–60.

———. "The Inquisition in Spanish Louisiana, 1762–1800." *New Mexico Historical Review* 50, no. 1 (January 1975): 45–72.

———. "The Mexican Inquisition and the Enlightenment, 1763–1805." *New Mexico Historical Review* 41, no. 3 (July 1966): 181–96.

Grimmelshausen, H.J.C. von. *The Adventures of Simplicius Simplicissimus.* Translated by A.T.S. Goodrick. Lincoln: University of Nebraska Press, 1962.

Groebner, Valentin. *Who Are You? Identification, Deception, and Surveillance in Early Modern Europe.* Translated by Mark Kyburz and John Peck. New York: Zone, 2007.

Guillén, Claudio. "Genre and Countergenre: The Discovery of the Picaresque." In *Literature as a System: Essays Toward the Theory of Literary History*, 135-58. Princeton, NJ: Princeton University Press, 1971.

——. "Toward a Definition of the Picaresque." In *Literature as a System: Essays Toward the Theory of Literary History*, 71-106. Princeton, NJ: Princeton University Press, 1971.

Hernández García, Jesús. *Fernández de Lizardi: Un educador para un pueblo.* Mexico: UNAM, 2003.

Herrero, Javier. "Renaissance Poverty and Lazarillo's Family: The Birth of the Picaresque Genre." *PMLA* 94, no. 5 (October 1979): 876-86.

Herzog, Tamar. *Defining Nations: Immigrants and Citizens in Early Modern Spain and Spanish America.* New Haven, CT: Yale University Press, 2003.

Homza, LuAnn. "Witch Hunting in Spain: The Sixteenth and Seventeenth Centuries." In *The Routledge History of Witchcraft*, edited by Johannes Dillinger, 134-44. London: Routledge, 2020.

Hyde, Lewis. *Trickster Makes This World: How Disruptive Imagination Creates Culture.* Edinburgh: Canongate, 2008.

Ikpi, Bassey. "What Bipolar II Feels Like." *New York Times*, July 6, 2019, Opinion section, https://www.nytimes.com/2019/07/06/opinion/sunday/bipolar-bassey-ikpi-book.html.

Israel, Jonathan I. *Radical Enlightenment: Philosophy and the Making of Modernity, 1650-1750.* Oxford and New York: Oxford University Press, 2002.

Jackson, Stanley. *Melancholia and Depression: From Hippocratic Times to Modern Times.* New Haven, CT: Yale University Press, 1986.

Jaffary, Nora E. *False Mystics: Deviant Orthodoxy in Colonial Mexico.* Lincoln: University of Nebraska Press, 2004.

Jiménez Salas, María. *Historia de la asistencia social en España en la Edad Moderna.* Madrid: Consejo Superior de Investigaciones Científicas, 1958.

Johnson, Carroll B. "Defining the Picaresque: Authority and the Subject in *Guzmán de Alfarache*." In *The Picaresque: Tradition and Displacement*, edited by Giancarlo Maiorino, 159-82. Minneapolis: University of Minnesota Press, 1996.

Johnson, Julie Greer. "Picaresque Elements in Carlos Sigüenza y Góngora's *Los Infortunios de Alonso Ramírez*." *Hispania* 64, no. 1 (March 1981): 60-67.

Kamen, Henry. "Toleration and Dissent in Sixteenth-Century Spain: The Alternative Tradition." *Sixteenth Century Journal* 19, no. 1 (Spring 1988): 3-23.

Keitt, Andrew W. *Inventing the Sacred: Imposture, Inquisition, and the Boundaries of the Supernatural in Golden Age Spain*. Leiden, the Netherlands, and Boston: Brill, 2005.

Lamadrid, Enrique. "The Rogue's Progress: Journeys of the Pícaro from Oral Tradition to Contemporary Chicano Literature of New Mexico." *MELUS* 20, no. 2 (Summer 1995): 15–34.

Leonard, Irving. *Books of the Brave: Being an Account of Books and of Men in the Spanish Conquest and Settlement of the Sixteenth-Century New World*. 2nd ed. New York: Gordian, 1964.

Lesage, Alain-René. *The Adventures of Gil Blas of Santillana*. Translated by Henri Van Laun. 3 vols. Edinburgh: William Paterson, 1886.

Levack, Brian, ed. *The Oxford Handbook of Witchcraft in Early Modern Europe and Colonial America*. New York: Oxford University Press, 2013.

Levine, Timothy R. *Duped: Truth-Default Theory and the Social Science of Lying and Deception*. Tuscaloosa: University of Alabama Press, 2019.

Lindberg, Gary. *The Confidence Man in American Literature*. New York: Oxford University Press, 1982.

López Lázaro, Fabio. "La mentira histórica de un pirata caribeño: el descubrimiento del transfondo histórico de *Los Infortunios de Alonso Ramírez* (1690)." *Anuario de Estudios Americanos* 64, no. 2 (July–December 2007): 87–104.

Lorente Medina, Antonio. *La prosa de Sigüenza y Góngora y la formación de la conciencia criolla mexicana*. Mexico: Fondo de Cultura Económica, 1996.

MacDonald, Michael. *Mystical Bedlam: Madness, Anxiety, and Healing in Seventeenth-Century England*. Cambridge, UK: Cambridge University Press, 1981.

MacKay, Ruth. *"Lazy, Improvident People": Myth and Reality in the Writing of Spanish History*. Ithaca, NY, and London: Cornell University Press, 2006.

Mancing, Howard. "The Protean Picaresque." In *The Picaresque: Tradition and Displacement*, edited by Giancarlo Maiorino, 273–91. Minneapolis: University of Minnesota Press, 1996.

Maravall, José Antonio. *La literatura picaresca desde la historia social (siglos XVI y XVII)*. Madrid: Taurus, 1986.

Martin, Norman F. *Los vagabundos en la Nueva España: Siglo XVI*. Mexico: Edit. Jus, 1957.

———. "Pobres, mendigos, y vagabundos en la Nueva España, 1702–1766: Antecedentes y soluciones presentados." *Estudios de Historia Novohispana* 8 (1985): 99–126.

Martínez, Miguel. *Front Lines: Soldiers' Writing in the Early Modern Hispanic World*. Philadelphia: University of Pennsylvania, 2016.

Martz, Linda. *Poverty and Welfare in Hapsburg Spain: The Example of Toledo*. Cambridge, UK: Cambridge University Press, 1983.

McCaa, Robert. "The Peopling of Mexico from Origins to Revolution." In *A Population History of North America*, edited by Michael R. Haines and Richard H. Steckel, 241–76. Cambridge, UK, and New York: Cambridge University Press, 2000.

McEnroe, Sean F. *A Troubled Marriage: Indigenous Elites of the Colonial Americas*. Albuquerque: University of New Mexico Press, 2020.

Melville, Herman. *The Confidence-Man: His Masquerade*. Evanston, IL: Northwestern University Press, 1984.

Menéndez Pidal, Ramón. *The Spaniards in Their History*. Translated by Walter Starkie. London: Hollis and Carter, 1950.

Midelfort, H. C. Erik. *A History of Madness in Sixteenth-Century Germany*. Stanford, CA: Stanford University Press, 1999.

———. *Mad Princes of Renaissance Germany*. Charlottesville: University Press of Virginia, 1994.

Mills, Kenneth R. "Mission and Narrative in the Early Modern Spanish World: Diego de Ocaña's Desert in Passing." In *Faithful Narratives: Historians, Religion, and the Challenge of Objectivity*, edited by Andrea Sterk and Nina Caputo, 115–31. Ithaca, NY: Cornell University Press, 2014.

———. "Ocaña's Mondragón and the 'Eighth Wonder of the World.'" In *Texts and Voices from Colonial and Postcolonial Worlds*. Edited by Arun W. Jones. College Park, PA: Penn State University Press, forthcoming.

———. "Una sacra aventura en tierras que se volvían santas: Diego de Ocaña, O.S.H., 1599–1608." *Allpanchis* (forthcoming).

Morales, Francisco. "Mexican Society and the Franciscan Order in a Period of Transition, 1749–1859." *The Americas* 54, no. 3 (January 1998): 323–56.

Nalle, Sara. *Mad for God: Bartolomé Sánchez, the Secret Messiah of Cardenete*. Charlottesville: University Press of Virginia, 2001.

Nesvig, Martin. *Promiscuous Power: An Unorthodox History of New Spain*. Austin: University of Texas Press, 2018.

———. "Religious Chicanery in Michoacán's Emergent Church." *Colonial Latin American Review* 17, no. 2 (December 2008): 213–32.

O'Hara, Matthew. "The Orthodox Underworld of Colonial Mexico." *Colonial Latin American Review* 17, no. 2 (December 2008): 233–50.

Otto, Rudolf. *The Idea of the Holy*. Translated by John W. Harvey. 2nd ed. Oxford and New York: Oxford University Press, 1958.

Owensby, Brian. *Empire of Law and Indian Justice in Colonial Mexico*. Stanford, CA: Stanford University Press, 2008.

Owensby, Brian, and Richard J. Ross, eds. *Justice in a New World: Negotiating Legal Intelligibility in British, Iberian, and Indigenous America*. New York: New York University Press, 2018.

Paris, Joel. *The Bipolar Spectrum: Diagnosis or Fad?*. New York and London: Routledge, 2012.

Parker, Charles H., and Gretchen Starr-LeBeau, eds. *Judging Faith, Punishing Sin: Inquisitions and Consistories in the Early Modern World*. Cambridge, UK, and New York: Cambridge University Press, 2017.

Pelton, Robert D. *The Trickster in West Africa: A Study of Mythic Irony and Sacred Delight*. Berkeley: University of California Press, 1980.

Pérez Marchand, Monelisa Lina. *Dos etapas ideológicas del siglo XVIII en México a través de los papeles de la Inquisición*. Mexico: El Colegio de México, 1945.

Pérez Moreda, Vicente. "The Plague in Castile at the End of the Sixteenth Century and Its Consequences." In *The Castilian Crisis of the Seventeenth Century*, edited by I. A. A. Thompson and Bartolomé Yun Casalilla, 32–59. Cambridge, UK: Cambridge University Press, 1994.

Piketty, Thomas. *Capital and Ideology*. Translated by Arthur Goldhammer. Cambridge, MA: Harvard University Press, 2020.

Porter, Roy. *Madness: A Brief History*. Oxford: Oxford University Press, 2002.

Quevedo, Francisco de. *La vida del buscón*. Edited by Fernando Cabo Aseguinolaza. Barcelona: Crítica, 1993.

———. *Lazarillo de Tormes and The Grifter: Two Novels of the Low Life in Golden Age Spain*. Translated by David Frye. Indianapolis: Hackett, 2015.

———. *Lazarillo de Tormes and The Swindler (El Buscón): Two Spanish Picaresque Novels*. Translated by Michael Alpert. London: Penguin, 2003.

Ramírez, Emma. "Ilustración y dominación: *El Periquillo Sarniento* bajo el Siglo de las Luces." *Revista de Humanidades: Tecnológico de Monterrey*, no. 21 (2006): 65-103.

Rosier Smith, Jeanne. *Writing Tricksters: Mythic Gambols in American Ethnic Fiction*. Berkeley: University of California Press, 1997.

Ruan, Felipe. "Literary History, Censorship, and Lazarillo de Tormes castigado." *Hispanic Research Journal* 17, no. 4 (2016): 269-87.

Sánchez Zapatero, Javier. "Heterogeneidad y fuentes literarias de *El Periquillo Sarniento* de José Joaquín Fernández de Lizardi." *Espéculo. Revista de Estudios Literarios*, no. 34 (2007): accessed at http://webs.ucm.es/info/especulo/numero34/psarnien.html.

Schwartz, Stuart B. *All Can Be Saved: Religious Tolerance and Salvation in the Iberian Atlantic World*. New Haven, CT: Yale University Press, 2008.

Sellers-García, Sylvia. *Distance and Documents at the Spanish Empire's Periphery*. Stanford, CA: Stanford University Press, 2013.

———. "Walking while Indian, Walking while Black: Modern Policing in a Colonial City." *American Historical Review* (forthcoming).

Shuger, Dale. *Don Quixote in the Archives: Madness and Literature in Early Modern Spain*. Edinburgh: Edinburgh University Press, 2012.

Sigüenza y Góngora, Carlos de. *Infortunios de Alonso Ramírez*. Mexico: Premia Editora, 1989. Originally published 1690.

———. *The Misfortunes of Alonso Ramírez (1690)*. Edited and translated by José F. Buscaglia-Salgado. New Brunswick, NJ: Rutgers University Press, 2019.

Simpson, Lesley B., ed. and trans. "The Spanish Crusoe: An Account by Maese Joan of Eight Years Spent as a Castaway on the Serrana Keys in the Caribbean Sea, 1528-1536." *Hispanic American Historical Review* 9, no. 3 (August 1929): 368-76.

Sinclair, David. *The Land That Never Was: Sir Gregor MacGregor and the Most Audacious Fraud in History*. Cambridge, MA: Da Capo, 2003.

Sisman, Adam. *The Professor and the Parson: A Study of Desire, Deceit, and Defrocking*. Berkeley, CA: Counterpoint, 2020.

Skirius, John. "Fernández de Lizardi y Cervantes." *Nueva Revista de Filología Hispánica* 31, no. 2 (1982): 257-72.

Slack, Paul. *The English Poor Law, 1531-1782*. Cambridge, UK, and New York: Cambridge University Press, 1995.

———. *From Reformation to Improvement: Public Welfare in Early Modern England*. Oxford: Oxford University Press, 1999.

Spell, Jefferson Rea. "The Intellectual Background of Lizardi as Reflected in *El Periquillo Sarniento*." *PMLA* 71, no. 3 (June 1956): 414–32.

———. *The Life and Works of José Joaquín Fernández de Lizardi*. Philadelphia: University of Pennsylvania Press, 1931.

———. *Rousseau in the Spanish World before 1833: A Study in Franco-Spanish Literary Relations*. Austin: University of Texas Press, 1938.

Tate, James. *Selected Poems*. Hanover, NH: University Press of New England for Wesleyan University Press, 1991.

———. *Selected Poems*. Middletown, CT: Wesleyan University Press, 2013.

Tawney, R. H. *The Agrarian Problem in the Sixteenth Century*. New York: Longmans, Green, 1912.

Taylor, William B. "Bandolerismo e insurgencia en el centro de Jalisco, 1790–1816." *Encuentro: Ciencias Sociales y Humanidades* 1, no. 3 (April–June 1984): 5–54.

———. *Theater of a Thousand Wonders: A History of Miraculous Images and Shrines in New Spain*. Cambridge, UK, and New York: Cambridge University Press, 2016.

Terpstra, Nicholas. *Cultures of Charity: Women, Politics, and the Reform of Poor Relief in Renaissance Italy*. Cambridge, MA: Harvard University Press, 2013.

Thomas, Hugh. *Conquest: Montezuma, Cortés, and the Fall of Old Mexico*. New York: Simon and Schuster, 1993.

———. *The Golden Empire: Spain, Charles V, and the Creation of America*. New York: Random House, 2010.

———. *Rivers of Gold: The Rise of the Spanish Empire*. London: Weidenfeld and Nicolson, 2003.

———. *World without End: Philip II and the First Global Empire*. New York: Random House, 2015.

Timmons, Wilbert H. *Morelos: Priest, Soldier, Statesman of Mexico*. El Paso: Texas Western College Press, 1963.

Torres Villarroel, Diego. *Vida, ascendencia, nacimiento, crianza y aventuras*. Edited by Guy Mercadier. Madrid: Clásicos Castalia, 1972.

Treviño Castro, Javier. "Síntoma de la urgente actualidad de la novela picaresca." *Vanguardia*, September 5, 2015, 1–4.

Vargas Llosa, Mario. "The Man Who Wasn't There." Book review of Javier Cercas's *The Impostor*. *Wall Street Journal*, August 28, 2018, https://www.wsj.com/articles/the-impostor-review-the-man-who-wasnt-there-1535060707.

Vargas Machuca, Bernardo de. *Milicia y descripción de las Indias*. Madrid: Pedro Madrigal, 1599.

Vega, Cristóbal de. *Casos raros de la confesión, con reglas y modo fácil para hacer una buena confesión general o particular*... Madrid: Viuda de Barco, 1812.

Vicens Vives, Jaime. *An Economic History of Spain*. Translated by Frances M. López-Morillas. Princeton, NJ: Princeton University Press, 1969.

Villa Flores, Javier. "Wandering Swindlers: Imposture, Style, and the Inquisition's Pedagogy of Fear in Colonial Mexico." *Colonial Latin American Review* 17, no. 2 (December 2008): 251–72.

Vogeley, Nancy. *Lizardi and the Birth of the Novel in Spanish America*. Gainesville: University Press of Florida, 2001.

Webb, Sidney. *English Poor Law History*. 3 vols. London: Longmans, 1927–63.

Zagorin, Perez. *Ways of Lying: Dissimulation, Persecution, and Conformity in Early Modern Europe*. Cambridge, MA: Harvard University Press, 1990.

Index